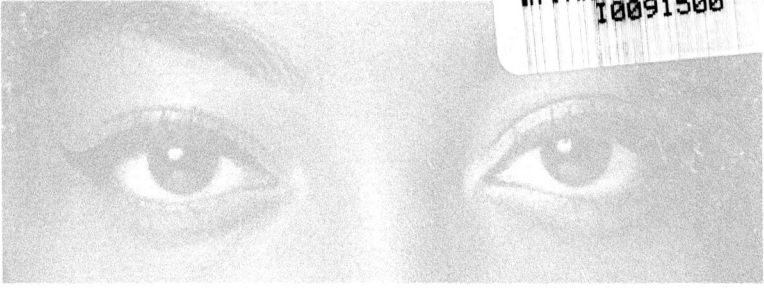

I DON'T
SEXUALLY
ABUSE
BLACK FEMALES

REV. DR. WALTER ARTHUR McCRAY—GOSPELIZER

I DON'T
SEXUALLY
ABUSE
BLACK FEMALES

BLACK CHRISTIAN BROTHERS AFFIRM MANDATE
TO SEXUALLY PROTECT OUR CULTURAL SISTERS

REV. DR. WALTER ARTHUR McCRAY—GOSPELIZER

BLACK LIGHT FELLOWSHIP
A Beacon of Christ
Chicago, Illinois

REV. DR. WALTER ARTHUR McCRAY is a Gospelizer, a holistic "Good News messenger" of the resurrected Lord, Jesus Christ. A seasoned minister, writer, national speaker, and servant-leader of the Church, he resides with his wife in Chicago.

I Don't Sexually Abuse Black Females

Black Christian Brothers Affirm Mandate to
Sexually Protect Our Cultural Sisters

REV. DR. WALTER ARTHUR McCRAY
Gospelizer

BLACK LIGHT FELLOWSHIP
A Beacon of Christ

Address: P.O. Box 5369 • Chicago, IL 60680
Phone: 773.826.7790 • FAX: 773.826.7792
Website: https://www.blacklightfellowship.com
Email: info@blacklightfellowship.com

Editorial Services:	Mary C. Lewis, MCL Editing, Etc., Chicago, IL
	mclwriter@msn.com
Cover Design:	TDB
	Clintswalkercolt@gmail.com

Printed in the U.S.A.   20 19 18   1 2 3 4 5

ISBN: 978-0-933176-29-4   Paper Edition
ISBN: 978-0-933176-30-0   eBook Edition

Printed on Acid-Free Paper.

Permissions

Books by Rev. Dr. Walter Arthur McCray

The Black Presence in the Bible (Vol. 1)
*Discovering the Black and African Identity
of Biblical Persons and Nations*

**The Black Presence in the Bible and The Table of Nations
Genesis 10:1-32 (Vol. 2)**
*With Emphasis on the Hamitic Genealogical Line
from a Black Perspective*

Pro-Black, Pro-Christ, Pro-Cross
African-Descended Evangelical Identity

The Black Presence and The Passion
A Christ-centered Historical Identity Response of a Gospelizer

Black Cherry Rising
Courage Facing A Spiritual Journey of Bittersweet Life and Change

Gospelizers!
Terrorized & Intensified

The African Wonder "Black Harry" Hoosier
A Gospelizer of Distinction

Black Young Adults
How to Reach Them, What to Teach Them

Get Grown! And Keep Growing
The Self-Help Adult Maturity Handbook

Marriage That Honors Divorce
When Breaking A Broken Union Pleases the Lord

The Christian Marriage Divorce Test™
A Guide for Assessing Whether to End Your Troubled Relationship

Sexually Sanctified Divorce
*How Spiritual Cleansing May Disrupt
Sexual Relations and Marriage*

Follow Jesus and MYOSB!
(Mind Your Own Spiritual Business!)

"Unity In Diversity Without Enforced Conformity"
Collaboration & Integrity of Activist Black Believers

A Rationale for Black Christian Literature
A Guide for Black Christian Writers and Authors –
The What? And the Why?

I Don't Sexually Abuse Black Females
Black Christian Brothers Affirm Mandate to
Sexually Protect Our Cultural Sisters

To order these and other titles, please visit

https://www.blacklightfellowship.com

For My Cultural Sisters . . .

violated, injured, blemished
by the sexual harm of callous males.

For your sexual and spiritual security . . .
coming in its full realization.

For your Brothers of African descent
to awaken with deep sexual sensitivity . . .
feeling the anguish of your feminine humanity . . .
protecting, aiding your redemptive healing.

For your sexual vindication—rightful, social, and restful . . .
bringing wholesome restoration . . .
manifesting high and holy aspirations of
your female Black personhood—body, mind, spirit, and soul . . .
of your precious, eternal being.

For your holistic sexual peace.

Rev. Dr. Walter Arthur McCray
May 10, 2018

Contents

III. Corrective Principles and Practices

I DON'T SEXUALLY ABUSE BLACK FEMALES

I.

Cultural
Problem and Protection

||||||||||||||||||||||||||||||||||||||||||||||||||||||||||||||||||||||

1

Sexual Abuse on Black Sisters

and

A Mandate for Brothers to Protect

◇◇

Moral outrage over male sexual abuse of females has risen, nationally and internationally. Notable stories of high-profile, American male, sexual abusers of females are a serious wake-up call—for white males, and, perhaps especially, for **Black males. Sexual assault happens to Black females at a higher rate than to their white counterparts.**[1]

Outcry of Sexually Abused American Females

Revelations of sexual scandals involving notable and powerful male figures began capturing the news cycle in 2017 and continues in 2018. The well-known news-breaking story of the conviction of "America's Dad" on three counts of aggravated indecent sexual assault is heartrending. The outcome of his gut-wrenching trial portends ominous consequences for any alleged sexual offenders—despite their power and influence—whose accusatory victims eventually get their day in court.[2]

Increasing news reports and trials have turned the moral, ethical, legally uncivil, and criminal spotlight on sexual misconduct, harassment, and assault, and on credible allegations of the same. Males who dominate and sexually exploit females are the key offenders, and some have acknowledged their sexual infractions. Other men are the subject of investigations into incidences of inappropriate sexual behavior and of illegal sexual activity, and some are in obstinate denial.

Sexual abuse perpetrators in the media, entertainment industry, and government are at the center of these explosive exposés. According to numerous credible witnesses, some contend that the highest office holder in the nation is not without moral, if not legal/criminal, culpability as a male sexual abuser. When coupled with his own self-confession in vulgarized words describing his extremely intentional and sexually assaulting behavior toward females, the accusations are quite plausible and condemning.[3]

Sexually Assaulted African-American Sisters

Aside from the high-profile cases, research and reports well establish that the sexual abuse perpetrated on females is widespread in American society, and it deeply affects innocent Black victims. Numerous women say that they have been sexually assaulted. In daily occurrences of American life, male sexual abuse of females abounds—in everything from **sexually degrading and demeaning communication, to sexual misconduct, sexual bullying and harassment, to girl-child molestation, to criminal sexual assault, to sex trafficking, to rape, to gang rape,** and more.

One in six women are victims of an attempted or completed rape in their lifetime. Annually, 1.3 million women may be victims of rape or attempted rape. More than 80% of all juvenile sexual victims are female. The overwhelming majority, 90%, of adult rape victims are female. Nearly 63% of women have experienced some form of sexual violence. **Blacks have a greater risk of rape or sexual assault** than any other racial/ethnic group except Native Americans. And the risk of experiencing sexual assault is even greater for low-income and urban Blacks.[4]

Sexually abused, but nevertheless courageous women are justifiably crying out for vindication. They are sending a wake-up call to males of all classes across America by widely casting their dragnet for sexual justice.[5] They desire to ensnare in public the secretive womanizers who lurk for sexual prey in all sectors of American life, including those male victimizers in diverse social, racial and religious groups. Our African-American Sisters especially are seeking shelter from male sexual violation. **Black and Christian men must hear, and take note.**

A Divine Voice and Warning

Spiritually attuned hearers appear to sense that a divine voice is raising the nation's collective consciousness about sexually abused females. Apparently, the Most High God of all humanity is sending a special moral message throughout the nation: males must cease their sexual abuse of females, and American society must hold fully accountable all sexual offenders of females.

Among others to whom He may be speaking, perhaps God is using the prevailing sexual issue to **prick the consciences** of Black males, especially by raising the consciousness of African-American men who follow Christ. Aside from God's dealings with others, my deeper convictions testify that Black Christian men—the "Brothers"—should begin to interpret the national reports and accusations of sexual abuse as **a divine warning** to Black male believers, and our churches.

The Sexual Mandate for Black Christian Brothers

Thus, might it be that in this season the Lord is specifically giving us Black Brothers the moral challenge to take care of our own sexual housekeeping? Isn't it quite plausible that God is provoking us to do a greater part in helping to clean up the sexual business in our own community and Christian relationships relative to females of African descent—our "Sisters"?[6]

I believe so, and promote this position.

I advocate that God has given Black Brothers a **sexual mandate**. As intuitively discerned, this sexual mandate is biblically based, spiritual, moral, and cultural. It is a mandate to advance Black male **sexual responsibility, integrity, and accountability** regarding the sexual abuse done to Black females. By His Spirit, the God of all humanity is divinely directing Black male believers to focus on attending to the sexual protection of the Sisters in our own cultural home. These are our women, our younger females, and our girls of African-American identity.

As Black men who are followers of Christ, God is moving African-American Christian men to stand especially against the injustices of **sexual abuse experienced by Black females at the hands of Black males**. Moreover, the Lord is compelling us as Brothers to **earnestly advocate for the effective prevention of Black male sexual abuse in our own circles of Christian faith**. This is essentially our divine sexual mandate. This is the immediate charge that God has given to Black Christian men in this hour of moral decision.

God is challenging and mandating Christ-centered Black men to commit ourselves to protecting our Sisters from Black male sexual violation **in all its forms**. He is pressing us as Brothers to spread a covering that safeguards Black females from sexual abuse that is either **spiritually immoral, uncivil, unethnical, unethical, or illegal**. Christian Black men must work to protect our Sisters from the full range of sexual abuse in all its degenerative and destructive manifestations.

In good measure, Black men who make personal and sexually responsible decisions have power to protect a vast number of Black females from sexual abuse and victimization. Many of these Sisters are active in our churches, and in our Christian organizations and connections. Black Christian men therefore have the power and moral influence to make a greater impact on remediating this social issue of sexually abused Black females. We are in a place of spiritual, cultural, and sexual responsibility, and of opportunity.

A Brother's Personal Affirmation

As Black Christian men we must rise to take our rightful ownership of this great sexual responsibility toward our Sisters. As Black

Brothers, we must seriously respond to the movement of God in the sexual affairs of our community. Therefore, I appeal to each African-American Christian man to **make the spiritual decision never to become, or to cease being, a sexual abuser of our Sisters**. Further, I encourage Black Christian Brothers to courageously articulate our commitment to obey God's sexual mandate, and advocate that we also take proactive steps to persuade all Black males under our influence to do the same. In terms that are passionate and unequivocal, here I state the personalized spiritual affirmation:

"I don't sexually abuse Black females."

The words of this affirmative commitment are intensely personal and courageous. The statement is more than a reflection on past conduct, "I *haven't* sexually abused Black females." Neither are these words a promise for future behavior, "I *won't* sexually abuse Black females." Instead, the words are an affirmation of the **present**, the right here and now, "I *don't* sexually abuse Black females."

— Apply the Affirmation —

Throughout life and in every circumstance,
as a Brother I responsibly choose to personally prevent
myself from committing any sexually abusive acts while in
the immediate presence, or whenever I contact a woman,
younger female, or girl-child. Any decision I make to
sexually protect our Sisters is current, and lasting.

Any Brother who makes this sexual affirmation—and resolves to stay true to his commitment—will empower and prevent himself from committing sexual abuse on our cultural females, our Sisters of

African descent. By applying biblical values and principles, as Black Christian men we can prevent ourselves from perpetrating immoral and illicit sexual behavior upon Black females.

❧

2

Focus on
Devalued Sister Sexual Victims
and
Brothers' Commitment to Protection

◇◇

Justified Regard for Black Female Sexual Victims

♦ **Focus**

Most stories of males' sexually abusing females that are receiving extensive exposure in the media deal with the cases and complaints of white women, not **Black women.**[7] **Our Sisters' experience is too**

often unjustifiably disregarded, minimized, or devalued in our society's coverage. In matters of sexual abuse, many often view the female factor as general and dominant, while they subsume the Black racial and ethno-cultural factors underneath the overall issue. Others focus on the holistic Black and female dimension of sexual abuse in the experience of African-descended Sisters. This discussion attempts the same. For reasons stated below, we call on Black Christian men to justifiably focus on addressing the sexual abuse issue of our cultural Sisters.

◆ Slavery

Historically and comparatively, females of African descent have suffered more sexual abuse in America than females of other groups. The **experience of Black chattel slavery** at the hands of whites in America—and its aftermath—by far accounts for the plethora of sexually abused Black women, female adolescents, and girls by white males. White males sexually abused Black females, and white slave owners forced Black males into sexual relationships with Black females. As pawns in the enslavers' system of economic exploitation, some Black males took advantage of the abusive sexual arrangements.[8]

The sexual abuse of Black females in slavery is a historical scourge upon America and the **white male** and **female** upholders of the dehumanizing system. In the past, society did not take Black female incidences of sexual violation legally or seriously, and the media underreported their experiences as sexual victims. The problems of dehumanization and disrespect of Black female life persists in America.

◆ Exclusion

In current times, there is a general exclusion of the Black female story of sexual abuse from the narratives of white American female sexual abuse. Whether the just causes of Black female victims of sexual abuse will rise with the current tide of public outrage against white male sexual abuse of white women is a matter of **wait-and-see**. Sexually abused Black women, younger females, and girls still have a long way to go for identification and vindication in American society.[9] Black female experiences and accounts of sexual abuse by white males, or by Black males, **struggles more for exposure, legal redress, and justice,** than do the occurrences of their white female counterparts.[10]

Some sexual victimizers threaten and intimidate their female victims to keep silent about the sexual abuse the women have suffered. Other sex offenders socially and immorally coerce female sexual victims into accepting "hush money." In startling cases across the U.S., some legal jurisdictions have failed to even process the medical evidence provided by rape victims.[11]

◆ Stories of Suffering Untold

Increasingly the mass media and social networks are spotlighting the very personal, embarrassing, and sordid stories of sexually violated female sufferers. Yet, it is not enough. The wider public never hears the numerous tell-all revelations that many Black and other female sexual victims eventually disclose in private counseling sessions, in small, close-knit groups, or in troublesome court cases. The silence of sexual incidences against Black females in underreported or never-reported cases is deafening. For every African-American woman who risks the compounded pain of reporting her rape ("blame-the-victim" Jezebel stereotype), **at least 15 African-American women do not report theirs.**[12]

Women—surely Black women—are tired, angry, and driven to advance the cause of exposing their male sexual abuse predators. They are beginning to push and reassert their cases of sexual abuse issues to the forefront of the news, and deeply into American consciousness. They rightfully do so. Many others must hear their stories. More men, a wider public, determined prosecutors, sensitive lawmakers, and discouraged Sister-victims must **hear the accounts of sexually abused females and their suffering:**

> sexually-related contracted diseases • physical trauma • ruined lives • broken careers • disrupted relationships • demoralized and demonized spirits • psychological scars • and more—all due to male sexual violations.

They must hear the stories and outcry of disgusted, yet hopeful and stronger, sexually abused female survivors.[13]

◆ Code of Silence

The African-American community, including Black believers and churches, have far too many of our share of cases dealing with females violated by sexual abuse. While we must carefully avoid the historical white stereotype that Black men are inherently sexual predators of white women,[14] we must also resist slipping into **denial** about the sexual abuse problems within our community.[15] Most Black men are not criminal sexual abusers of Black females, but the females of our community experience too many cases of male sexual abuse.

For a variety of reasons, Black believers and churches, Christian circles, organizations, and families keep quiet about many of their male sexual scandals. Pathetically, **a sexual abuse code of silence** influences the African-American community and certain sectors of Black Christian faith.[16] As individual believers, African-American male followers of Christ should not seek to skirt this problematic and prevalent sexual issue. In the matter of sexual abuse—especially on Black females—none of us Black Christian men can conveniently hide beneath the cultural covers of "racism," "the system," "injustice," "oppression," "for the cause," "lack of social and economic opportunities," or the like. Attempts to justify our silence or inaction on these grounds just doesn't work. In this matter, our social reality is **a moral Black-male-on-Black-female sexual issue**.

Brothers' Cultural Commitment to Sisters' Sexual Protection

♦ Step Up

Despite the cover of silence, and its shame, God calls Black Christian men to address this socially hot discussion, and the sexual state of affairs in our community, in an open and straight up manner. The male sexual abuse of females in African-American relationships is a spiritual, community, and cultural problem—not just a societal problem. Instead of acquiescing to the sexual code of silence in our community, **Black Christian men must step up to change the Black male's code of sexual misconduct toward Black females**.

The historical and contemporary experiences of Black female victims of sexual abuse are major reasons that Christian Black men should protect females of African descent from becoming sexual victims. Black men must not emulate and perpetuate white male patterns of sexually abusing Black females, past or present. We must always resist acting the part of our oppressors in their sexually unrighteous practices: *"Do not envy the oppressor, And choose none of his ways"* (Proverbs 3:31, NKJV). As Black men who profess Christ, **we must be the very last male group in American society that** entertains even a passing thought to commit sexual abuse on any **Black female**.

♦ Commit

I believe that God's prophetic voice is calling Christian males of African descent to **commitment**. By faithful obedience we must heed the divine call and accept the sexual-social challenge of our day. The holiness of the God that we serve obligates Black male believers to respond to the changing sexual attitudes and social transformations taking place in our society and community. God expects us to step up our game. The time has arrived for us to take decisive action in this sexually moral moment by making a clear and unequivocal stand for sexual justice.

In the arena of sexual interrelations, as Black Christian men we must demonstrate **personal righteousness** and **civility**, must show **cultural compassion**, and must promote **justice** and **vindication** for our sexually violated Sisters. And—in the Name of our Lord Jesus Christ—each of us must advance this righteous cause by affirming a personal commitment: **"I don't sexually abuse Black females."**

Affirmative Words and Preventive Actions

♦ A Practical Discussion

The spiritual affirmation cited above anchors this entire discussion. It is a personal response to a divine mandate. It is a practical means by which each Brother can **take personal ownership** of the sexual abuse problem that negatively impacts our own women, our male ranks, and our community's progress. The obvious aim of this affirmation is to help our Brothers to prevent and rectify the sexual abuse experienced by Black Sisters—a not infrequent immoral and/or illegal practice in our community, and in society. As implied above, culture and faith give context to this Black and Christian perspective, which focuses on the key role of African-American male believers in addressing the issue of female sexual abuse by males in the Black community.

◆ Biblical Ideas

Specific biblical ideas inform this Black Christian perspective. Here you have a practical **biblical approach** for curtailing the sexually abusive behavior of Black males. The approach supplies protective solutions to help you as a Brother to remedy the sexual abuse problem facing many Black Sisters. **Word-based principles** appear in this discussion, several in the straightforward form of seven sexual affirmations and seven sexually-related guidelines.

◆ Affirmations and Actions

If you feel the urgent need, we encourage you to go directly to **"Corrective Principles and Practices"** (part III), and read there first. There you will find biblical explanations and applications for your immediate use. Apply these principles to protect those Sisters who are in your life, and under your influence, from sexual violations. Affirm and practice these guidelines to guard yourself from doing any sexually abusive thing that could result in civil or legal repercussions.

Here are the affirmations:

1) † "I am sexually **spiritual**."

2) † "I am sexually **moral**."

3) † "I am sexually **civil**."

4) † "I am sexually **ethnical**."

5) † "I am sexually **ethical**."

6)   † "I am sexually **legal**."

7)   † "I am sexually **protectoral**."

Here are the seven sexually-related **relationship practices** that a Brother should apply in his interactions with the Sisters:

First   ◊ Practice sexual **Consecration** as a primary virtue.

Second ◊ Promote **Community** in male-female relations.

Third   ◊ Use clear **Communication** on sexual matters.

Fourth ◊ Keep **Control** of your sexual urges and conduct.

Fifth   ◊ Follow your **Conscience** in sexual gray areas.

Sixth   ◊ Take **Confession** of sexual sins seriously.

Seventh ◊ Make a **Covenant** with your eyes for sexual purity.

By applying these principles and practices, you manifest a sincere determination and effort as a Black male believer—as a Brother who desires to make a social difference and change by **positively reordering sexual interrelations** between Black males and Black females, and **maintaining sexually responsible behavior**. The biblical affirmations and practices that you observe can assist you in **demonstrating personal integrity** as a Christ-centered Black man who honestly confronts the issue of sexually protecting Black females, our Sisters.

◆ Perspective and Purpose

The second section is **"Christian Perspective and Prophesying"**. Here you will find an in-depth understanding of "sexual abuse," integrated with biblical ideas and solutions. There is also an expanded discussion of unethical sexual practices of Black men, and the meaning of **our sexual integrity as Brothers**, even as Black men who follow Christ.

Protective Purpose and Outcomes

Overall, this discussion aims to motivate and empower us as Christian Black Brothers to provide a **greater measure of sexual protection**, first for our Sisters—with the goal that each one can freely relate to any of us without fear of sexual threats or abuse—and consequently, for ourselves—with the goal that none of us commit moral, civil, or criminal sexual violations.

❧

II.

Christian
Perspective and Prophesying

IIIIIIIIIIIIIIIIIIIIIIIIIIIIIIIIIIIIIIIIIIIIIIIIIIIIIIIIIIIIIIIIIIIIIIIIII

3

Sexual Abuse Definition
and
Christian Biblical Ideas

◇◇◇

Understand "Sexual Abuse," Legally

♦ Harm

Sharpening our understanding of the definitive nature of "sexual abuse" is helpful. Generally, sexual "abuse" is sexual "harm," "mistreatment," or "misuse" of a person. It is undesired, unwanted, and unsafe sexual behavior by one (usually stronger) person upon another (weaker). The abuser's inappropriate, indecent, or worse behavior may be by contact or in activity, or by attempting such conduct upon a nonconsenting person. It may be an overt act, or a subtle manipulation. Sexual abuse may happen as an isolated event, or a repeated practice.[17]

♦ Uncivil and Criminal

Laws related to sexual crimes can differ from state to state. As a rule that legally defines its uncivil and criminal nature, consider that **sexual abuse**—as **harassment, intimidation, sexism, homophobic mistreatment, molestation, assault, rape,** and the like—covers inappropriate, sexually-related or -motivated gestures, speech, or actions, control or manipulation. Sexual abuse is sexual misconduct, exploitation, or battery. It can be threatening, forceful, and drug- and alcohol-induced sexually-related assault. This includes rape and date rape (i.e., unwanted vaginal, oral, or anal penetration), sexual slavery and trafficking, and other forms of physical sexual violence. Some types of domestic violence include the sexual assault or rape of one's spouse, or intimate partner.[18]

♦ Power, Not Love

Sexual abuse is not an act of pleasure or passionate love. Sexual abuse is an immoral, illegal, harmful, and harsh sexual expression of **power, authority, control, aggression, oppression,** or **violence**—but is not an expression of genuine love. Sexual abuse attacks the victims' physical and psychological integrity, and their dignity, respect, and security. Sexual abuse is a hostile and destructive act.

♦ Scope and Impact

Consider the wide spectrum and impact of sexual abuse. The scope of sexually abusive behavior covers many persons and classes. Sexual abuse shows its destructive face across the world; from women to men; from children to elders; from girls to boys; from spouses to singles; from parents to siblings; from persons with developmental disabilities to persons with dementia; from majorities to minorities; from churches and religious groups[19] to private and public entities in society; from direct personal contact to indirect personal contact via digital communication.

In American society there are sexually abused females (by males and females); sexually abused children (by adults they know and trust); sexually abused males (by men and women); sexually abused wives and husbands (by their spouse); sexually abused elders (by someone younger); sexually abused dependents (by their caretakers or guardians), sexually abused patients (by their doctors or medical caregivers), sexually abused stepchildren (by a stepparent in a blended family), etc.

All these persons and entities may experience sexual abuse in a variety of ways, and certainly the victims face related issues, consequences, and effects on their life and future well-being.[20] The specific focus of this conversation is on sexually abused Black females. Our task is to help prevent the male sexual abuse of women, younger females, and little girls—to sexually protect Black females from the abusive behavior of Black males.

Highlight Sexual Abuse, Biblically

♦ Biblical, Holistic Definition

This is a Christian and biblical perspective on male **"sexual abuse."** Christian biblical definitions and descriptions of abusive sexual behavior cover and prohibit a wider range of abusive sexual acts and behaviors than "civil" and "criminal" legal definitions. Our society's standards of accountability in areas of sexual behavior are usually lower than Scripture-taught divine standards for a person's sexual "spirituality."

```
┌─────────────────────────────────────────────────────────────┐
│              Sexual Abuse on a Legal Continuum               │
│                                                             │
│  Not Illegal  ————————— Legally Uncivil ————————— Criminal  │
│                                                             │
│  Sexual Rudeness —— Sexual Harassment —— Sexual Assault/Rape │
└─────────────────────────────────────────────────────────────┘
```

This discussion is **holistic**, in that it attempts to shine a biblically-defined spotlight on all sexually abusive/harmful behavior by Black males, whether illegal or not. In an overall Christian perspective, Scripture expositors can make the case that believers should classify all forms of sexual abuse (by males or by females) as sexually "unspiritual"/"immoral." Sexually unspiritual/immoral behaviors are sinful, and are inherently harmful either to another or to oneself, whether the behaviors are illegal or lawful (cf. biblical lists of sexual sins, Mark 7:21; Romans 1:24; 1 Corinthians 6:9; Galatians 5:19; Ephesians 4:19; Colossians 3:5, etc.).

In the eyes of God's law (that is, His commandments and spiritual standards as biblically defined), any sexually unholy and immoral perceptions or behavior expressed by a male toward a female is abusive. Biblically speaking, "sexual abuse" may cover anything that is **sexually unspiritual/immoral**, ranging from a person's **thoughts**,[21] to their **communication** to their **conduct**. Thus, in this conversation, **"sexual abuse"** covers more than a male's illegal sexual activity involving a female, whether he has violated civil or criminal laws.

♦ **Spiritual Harm**

For instance, on the one hand, a male's **words** may be sexually vulgar and harmful to a female; but they are not necessarily illegal. On the other hand, a male's sexual **actions** on a female may indicate violent sexual assault or rape, which certainly are harmful and criminal. Though one behavior is illegal, and the other is not, each of these occurrences are instances of male "sexual abuse." Both cause "harm" to a female in its own way. Such behavior even may harm others in a relationship to the female. For example, consider the harm brought to young boys and girls who witness inappropriate sexual conversation or a sexual assault—whether verbal or physical—on their mother or another Black female. In either case, the behavior of the male sexual abuser is damaging to the lives of the female and those impressionable children.

Brothers must **cease and avoid all manner of sexual abuse/ harm** committed on Black females, whether the sexual behavior flies under the legal radar or is straight-up criminal. A Black male should never take pleasure in sexually abusive behavior simply because what he sexually does to a Sister is permissible or non-prosecutable in the eyes of the law. **All sexual abuse is spiritually harmful.** And spiritual harm is great harm, and is subject to divine retribution.

◆ Ambitious Sexual Values

This Christian biblical approach to correcting male sexual abuse unapologetically advocates ambitious sexual values and spiritual standards for Black men who confess Jesus Christ. God's Word commands us as Brothers to step up our game in the sexual arena of life. He commands us to hold one another accountable for our sexual behavior as Brothers who fellowship in churches and Christian circles.

For certain, as Brothers we must all keep ourselves **legal** by never committing legally uncivil or criminal sexual activities. All of us must consistently show **civility** in our gender-to-gender expressions, manners, and behavior. And we do ourselves well as Black Christian men when we strive to continually please God by becoming sexually **spiritual** in all our thoughts and ways, both in private and in public.

Characterize Sexually Abusive Behaviors

♦ Terms of Abuse

Several familiar terms characterize the essence of the harmful behavior of a sexually abusive person. Consider **"unspiritual,"** **"immoral," "uncivil," "unethical,"** and **"illegal"/ "criminal."** Alongside these, I believe that sexual abuse is also **"unethnical"**— indicating that this sexually abusive behavior brings **harm to one's ethno-cultural group**; in this context, to the African-American group.

"Unethnical" sexual behavior is an expression of the abusive sexual conduct that Black males do to Black females. Or it is how non-Black males focus on sexually targeting Black females precisely because they are Black or African-American (cf. the sexual experience of African-Americans during their slavery experience by whites; or, hate crimes and sexual violence directed against a specific racial group or class). This type of sexual abuse on Black females is anti-cultural to the overall progress of African-American people since it is destructive of Black Sisters, and/or of their relationships to Black men, in the context of a people of African descent in America.

Describing a Range of Sexually Abusive Behavior

"Unspiritual"—"Immoral"—"Uncivil"—"Unethnical"—"Unethical"—"Illegal"/"Criminal"

Christian ——————————— Cultural ——————————— Societal

V   A   L   U   E   S

♦ Overlapping Consequences

Characteristics of sexually abusive behavior often overlap, and at times one characteristic of sexual abuse may have consequences in another area. Consider how these characteristics of sexual abuse can play out in different instances when male abuse of females is apparent.

❖ When "Immoral" is "Uncivil"

- For instance, a male's **"immoral"** sexual behavior (such as exposing himself to a female co-worker), or his obscene intrusive talk about personal sexual experiences, may result in **"civil"** consequences for demonstrating this "unethical" behavior: "You're fired!"

❖ When "Unethical" is "Illegal"/"Criminal"

- When the agencies, institutions, and businesses of a society are **"civil,"** they treat some forms of sexual abuse as both **"unethical"** and **"illegal"/"criminal."** For example, we can refer to the relationship of a male administrative superior to a female subordinate worker, which may result in a pressured and **"unethical"** sexual arrangement related to securing her gainful employment. Or the relationship may lead to some form of sexual harassment like repeated and unsolicited sexual advances in the workplace—an **"illegal"** practice.

❖ When "Immoral" is "Criminal"

- In all states, legal authorities can bring **"criminal"** charges against a sexually **"immoral"** and overbearing husband for sexually assaulting or raping his own wife, despite the fact that the laws in some states make it difficult for the victim to prove her case.[22] He may think, erroneously, that the laws of marriage grant him absolute control over his wife's body, or the right to have her perform all kinds of uncomfortable sexual tricks.

❖ When "Unethical" is "Criminal"

- Having unprotected sex is **"unethical"** and abusive when there is a known danger of exposing one's partner to a sexually transmitted disease (as some Black males have done to their Sisters). In some occurrences, when a sex partner fails to disclose personal health facts that are vital and potentially harmful, the practice of having unprotected sex is **"illegal,"** both **"uncivil"** and **"criminal."** The offender is liable for civil damages and/or prosecution for his unsafe practices.[23]

❖ When "Unspiritual" is "Criminal"

- When we say that a Black male is sexually **"unspiritual"** or **"immoral"** (e.g., a fornicator) this description may also lead to identifying him as sexually **"criminal."** For example, because he exploits or manipulatively engages in sexual activities with a female child (like exposing his genitals, or photographing a child in sexual poses, or touching the child's private parts). Or the immoral male may entertain himself with pornographic photos of underaged girls (a sex crime).

❖ When "Not Illegal" is "Unethnical"

- It is not **"illegal"** for a Black man to take full advantage as often as possible of a Black female sexual partner. But it is certainly **"immoral"** and **"unethnical"** for him not to marry the Sister when she desires a marital union, and no legal or justifiable impediments exist to prevent her man—her continual sex partner—from doing the righteous thing by marrying an available Black woman. He should marry the Sister and form a Black family. Or he should immediately quit sexually and socially misusing/abusing her and her wonderful African body.

❖ When "Not Illegal" is "Morally Uncivil"

- Certain sexually degrading references to Black females in the lyrics of some popular songs are sexually **"unethnical"** from the viewpoint of a Black identity and cultural perspective. Likewise, so are the callous and desecrating sex conversations of profane Black men about our Sisters. Though not **"illegal"** in most cases, the sexually abusive conduct reflected in the vulgar and disrespectful language that targets Black women (i.e., street sexual harassment) is **"morally uncivil,"** and is also **"ethnically"** abusive (or is **"sexually unethnical"**) for Black females and our people.

❖ When "Legally Civil" is "Unspiritual"

- According to laws currently in force, not all forms of **"unspiritual," "immoral,"** or **"unethnical"** sexual behavior are necessarily legally **"uncivil," "unethical,"** or **"criminal."** For example, males may legally view female adult pornography; or, in some jurisdictions of Nevada they may legally use the service of a prostitute. Moreover, numerous strip clubs, sex shops, adult movie theaters, adult video arcades, peep shows, sex shows, and sex clubs enjoy legal protections and abound across the nation.

In addition to the above, there certainly are other examples and instances of overlapping characteristics and consequences of sexually abusive male behavior.

Contrasting Perspectives on Sexual Abuse

Biblical Standards	Societal Standards
Harmful	Harmful
but	**and**
Legal	Illegal
Sexual Behavior	Sexual Behavior
According to Scripture	**According to Laws**
Abusive	Abusive
Sexual Behavior	Sexual Behavior
may be	**is definitely**
Non-Criminal/Legal	Illegal/Criminal

Biblically,

Sexual Abuse

covers any

Thoughts or Behavior

that are

SEXUALLY HARMFUL

Conceptualizations ———— Communications ———— Conduct

Brothers should view Sexual Abuse as . . .

"Unspiritual" — "Immoral"—

— "Uncivil" — "Unethnical" —

— "Unethical" — "Illegal"/"Criminal"

Contrasting Examples of Sexually Related/Abusive Biblical Sins and Societal Practices

◊ **Examples of biblically unspiritual, immoral, uncivil, sexual sins; some are illegal but seldom prosecuted:**

- lustful sexual gazing
- vulgar and obscene sex talk/ words
- sexual joking and teasing
- adult pornography
- fornication
- adultery
- unwarranted divorce/adultery
- sexual orgies
- lusts, passions
- lasciviousness
- male or female prostitution
- etc.

◊ **Examples of legally uncivil, unethical, and criminal sexual expressions and practices:**

- sexual bullying
- sexually exposing oneself
- sexual harassment in workplace
- girl/child molestation
- sexual assault and battery, rape, gang rape
- sexual slavery and trafficking
- sexual blackmail and abuse of power
- sexual stalking
- subtle manipulation and bribery of a child for sexual purposes
- threatening to harm a child, or to withdraw love and affection from her, with the intent to sexually engage the minor girl
- etc.

Classify Actual/Potential Male Sexual Abusers

♦ Three Categories

Potential or actual sexually abusive males may generally fall into either of three broadly defined categories.[24] Considering sexual abuse, a male (1) has acted abnormally by committing an incidental act of sexual abuse; (2) is a clinically sick and unhealthy chronic perpetrator of sexual abuse; or (3) may have never sexually abused. There are different approaches and solutions for addressing the problems of these male sexual abusers or offenders. At the outset, however, we should beware that short of an abuser's death or complete social isolation, no single method of preventing a male from sexually violating a female is 100% foolproof.[25]

♦ Clinically Unhealthy

According to the diagnoses and practices of clinicians, **some male sexual abusers are very unhealthy**. The reasons these males sexually abuse females is due to the males having deep-rooted mental, psychological, or emotional problems.[26] Simply, they are sick or ill, and need the professional services of an appropriate doctor. Often, these sexual abusers are offenders in the legal sense. Consequently, counteracting and healing their sexually abusive behavior requires a range of intensive treatment. This may include professional counseling, therapy, medication, and other measures to protect potential female targets from becoming the sexual prey of a habitual offender.

♦ Abnormally Acting

In contrast, **other male sexual abusers act abnormally but are not necessarily clinically unhealthy**. Perhaps spontaneously in a single incident, these otherwise "normal" men simply have acted impulsively and irresponsibly without showing discretion for a female in a social and sexual matter. Correcting the abusive sexual behavior of these abnormally acting men requires that those who have major influence over these incidental offenders should firmly hold them accountable for the uncivil or criminal act of sexual abuse they committed. These sexual victimizers may require some form of general counseling and/or should make repair for their criminal or legally uncivil behavior. But they do not necessarily need clinical treatment or medication.

♦ Potentially Abusive

Most Black males have never committed criminal sexual abuse on any female. Despite that, the likelihood of arrest for violent crimes by African-Americans is approximately six times the arrest rates of whites.[27] However, **any male, *per se,* is a potential sexual abuser of a female**, in ways that are criminal or non-criminal. The task is to guard non-abusers from ever entering the ranks of actual sexual abusers of females. Gaining a Black man's commitment to spiritual values in the sexual area of life has a lot to do with preventing him from committing sexual abuse on Black females. Education from a genuine Black Christian perspective, and the cultural reinforcement of a responsible community, are keys to reaching the goal of helping sexually non-abusive males to remain sexually responsible and non-offensive by staying the spiritual course.

Offer Biblically Responsible Solutions

♦ Good Decisions

This discussion courageously presents biblical ideas as a remedy for helping to prevent the sexual violation of females by any male, *per se*. By attempting to stop or prevent the sexual abuse that Black males do to Black females, **the approach at hand offers practical and redemptive solutions for any male who can make responsible**

choices, to whatever degree he is capable. To a good extent, most abusive males can make responsible decisions by choosing or refusing a specific course of sexual behavior. Hence, abusive males in either category can responsibly apply to life positive teachings and instructions that are good for correction and character building. This includes using biblical and spiritual solutions that address problems of sexual abusers, even when used in combination with other kinds of remedies.

◆ Integrated Approach

Black Christian professionals and clinicians often take an integrated approach in counseling, treating, and correcting the behaviors of sexual abusers. With their best clinical practices, they combine biblical values, personal spirituality, and the support of Christian community to help their clients resolve sexual problems. The outcomes of adopting **a holistic approach**—which is a very Christian perspective—are often very beneficial.

◆ Spiritual Support

Intercessory **prayers**, and a close-knit **support group**, can be very effective in correcting unspiritual and immoral sexual behavior. In addition, some sexually abusive men will receive help primarily through the spiritual power of **deliverance** from sexual sins, or by the ministry of exorcism from demonic influences. In this regard, the deliverance ministries found in many churches may become a vital solution for correcting the anti-female and destructive behavior of some male sexual abusers.

◆ Biblical Teachings

Biblically-based instruction and counseling is always advisable for those men whose sexual behavior deviates from spiritual, moral, civil, ethnical, ethical, or legal standards. Christian teachings are useful for nurturing and maintaining upright sexual behavior, or for preventing or correcting sexually abusive inclinations or practices. Black Christian men should make use of biblical ideas as a personal defense against committing sexual abuse upon our female relations.

Used wisely, biblical principles can **prevent the outbreak** of potential sexually abusive actions by any Brother whose motivations about sexual matters are wholesome and well-intentioned. In addition, insights and wisdom from God's Word can assist an offending Brother in **overcoming sexually abusive patterns** of behavior, including sexual criminal activity.

4

Unethnical Sexual Practices
and
Black Brothers of Integrity

◇◇◇

Black Male
Ethno-Cultural Sexual Abuse
of Sisters

♦ Sexual Greed

In some cases, sexual looseness or addiction drives Black males to exploit Black women, Christian women—any woman. They treat a community of Sisters as a sexual harem, and avail themselves of every opportunity to sleep around (or to shack up) with their sexual choice for the occasion or season.

This conduct is a prime example of male sexual abuse characterized as **"unethnical."** In this context, the term indicates sexually abusive behavior that brings harm to Black females and thereby to the Black ethno-cultural group of African-Americans. "Unethnical" sexual behavior is an expression of the abusive sexual conduct that Black males do to Black females. The "unethnical" sexual issue treated here speaks to behavior and practices of those Black males who, biblically speaking, are **immorally guilty of sexual greed.** We read in Ephesians 4:19-20, *"[19] They have become callous and have given themselves up to sensuality, greedy to practice every kind of impurity. [20] But that is not the way you learned Christ!"* (*ESV*, cf. the association of "greediness" and "idolatry" with sexual sins in Galatians 5:19, Ephesians 5:3, Colossians 3:5, etc.).

♦ **Distrustful Relationships**

Unethnical sexual practices raise the issue of **trust** for all who desire genuine community in the Black ethno-cultural experience. For instance, in the African-American community we may ask, **how healthy and high is the trust factor between Black males and Black females**? Or, what major part do sexual ideas and relations have to do with building or destroying trust and community relationship between Black men and Black women?

Any Black man who sexually manipulates, controls, violates, or exploits a Black female is **not a trustworthy "brother,"** Christian or not. By sexually objectifying Black females, such a "brother" thereby demonstrates that he is not truly serious about bringing holistic progress and justice to Black people. At the least, his immoral actions bring his deeper motivations and values into serious question. The irresponsible sexual behavior of **some Black males, and especially**

of certain community leaders, destroys the trust relationship between Black males and Black females.

Wholesome relationships of Black males and Black females, especially their marital relationships, are the greatest community and social asset of African-American people. The behavior of Black males who relate in abusively sexual ways to Black females destroys this asset. These kinds of sexual hookups destroy **trust** between the sexes, disrupt good relationships between Sisters, and they further undermine genuine community for Black people. Such sexual practices are ethically immoral and **culturally counterproductive**.

Sexually abusive behavior of Black males (whether viewed as lawful or illegal sexual conduct), and the resultant **distrust** it produces between Black males and Black females, is a cultural problem. The problem is obvious in nonconsensual sexual relations such as child molestation, sexual assault, or rape.

♦ Consensual Exploitation

However, the cultural problem of sexual abuse also manifests even when some partners participate in **consensual sexual activity**. For instance—and surely not blaming the victim—some sexually abused women are emotionally unhealthy. By sexually submitting to male manipulation and domination—characteristics of sexual abuse—they reveal their vulnerability. Instead of resisting the undesired sexual advances of unwanted males, the Sisters reluctantly give sexual consent.

Consequently, those men who are immoral and cruel **seize every opportunity to take repeated and full sexual advantage of Sisters** who demonstrate spiritual, psychological, social, and sexual weaknesses. Though the parties in this type of sexual liaison are "consenting adults," the intimate relationship is nonetheless sexually abusive. In this relationship, the Black female party is a controlled sexual victim of the Black male who abuses and misuses the Sister (cf. 2 Timothy 3:6-7).

Victims of abuse (sexual or otherwise) often willingly submit to the offensive behavior of the perpetrator. This response to social mistreatment is a typical psychological and self-defeating pattern of submission by an oppressed person. The abusive situation often requires an outside intervention to break the destructive cycle and the psychological control wielded by the victimizer over the victim under bondage. Similar dynamics of male control take place in the prostitution relationship of sex workers to the sexual predators/handlers who dominate and pimp weakened women and young girls. **Emotional weakness and psychological bondage** are present in some relationships of males who sexually abuse Black females.

Whether or not a Sister consensually and "freely" participates with a Black man in his (or their) sexual exploits, the reprehensible conduct of these males is describable in no other terms but sexually and morally **"ethnical abuse."** Society does not usually treat a man's (or woman's) fornication or adulterous behavior as illegal or criminal. However, the conduct is certainly unspiritual, and is sexually and morally corrupt.

◆ Marital Disrespect

For unjustified reasons, many sexually promiscuous and unethnical Black men refuse to marry, or to stay faithfully married to a faithful Sister. Oftentimes single Black males with these sexual characteristics father children, but fail to marry either of their children's mothers. On the other hand, married males of this kind also father extra-marital children. A scandal may erupt. Sometimes the adulterous acts lead to civil actions against the perpetrator for his immoral and unethical sexual behavior. Also, the wife of the adulterer becomes a female victim of her husband's extra-marital abusive sexual behavior, and may seek legal recourse.

◆ Irresponsible Leaders

Regretfully, sexual irresponsibility of leaders at high social levels has invaded or manifested itself in the ranks of the Black community. The list includes Christian ministers, religious leaders, organizational heads, community activists, business owners, and other influential men in African-American circles.

The community publicly commends some Black men and Brothers for prophetically beating the vocal drums of Black freedom, opportunity, and empowerment. Through the grapevine, however, the community also knows that some of our prophetical leaders simultaneously act in immoral ways that sexually disrespect and misuse Black females. Some relate to our Sisters in ways that **perpetuate a social status of female subservience**, a door that often may easily lead to other forms of female sexual abuse.

◆ Scandalous Damage

Consequently, some African-American leaders cast aside moral restraints and professional ethics to exploit numerous sexual opportunities with the Sisters in our community. This immoral behavior pattern gets these male leaders into scandalous trouble. Sexual illegalities of Black male leaders, and credible allegations lodged against them, often become a great embarrassment and setback for their followers, and for the general progress of Black people.

The damaging results of unethical and unethnical sexual abuse by Black males in leadership positions is telling:

---

an obscene mentoring model of abandoning oneself to sexual promiscuity • extra-marital sexual relationships • children born out of wedlock • family disruption • social scandal • disdain of Black leadership • loss of credibility • mockery by our enemies • and weakened work and ministry.

Due to Black male leaders who have been sexually irresponsible and unaccountable, the African-American community, churches, various groups, and families have all experienced the degenerating and painful effects of sexual transgressions and the resultant social disgrace. Sexually victimized Black females suffer most.

♦ **Anti-Female Behavior**

Unquestionably, sexually irresponsible ways of Black males are destructive of Black females, family, and community. Sexual abuse by Black men on Black women is **anti-female** and **anti-womanhood**. Abusive Black sexual behaviors on Black women are **anti-cultural**. Unethnical sexual practices by Black males, with their dire consequences, work against a Black female's every good spiritual fiber, her cultural esteem, and her personal and social well-being.

Question: In the experience of a Black female who lives and relates to Brothers in a sexually unethnical toxic environment that sexually irresponsible Black males carelessly foment—**within a social context of high distrust**—how in God's world is it possible for her as a woman of African descent to continually thrive in doing her vital mission for God and her family, and be of service to her community?

Black men who manifest sexual greed are exploitatively abusive of Black women. We must note them for their sexually immoral corrupt fruit, and deal with them accordingly. All those in Black circles who mean well should avoid male sexual victimizers, strive to deliver them, or should seek to effectively and socially neutralize them for their unspiritual, immoral, and unethnical sexual practices.

♦ **Protective Prophets**

Black Christian male leaders and social activists must attain a deeper sense of sexual responsibility, according to the biblical traditions of our prophetic predecessors. For the greater part, prophets in biblical time periods, and in the spiritual stream of the earliest Church, were not sexually immoral. Prophets in both the Old and New Covenant communities treated **females with a sense of sexual sacredness, and protection**. Contemporary Black social prophets of Christ ought to nurture the same spirit of sexual holiness toward Black females.

Black Christian males who take up the cause to despise, confront, and struggle against the social abuse and oppression of white people against African-American people, must also learn to respect, and to bestow sexual protection, social freedom, and spiritual honor upon the lives of our Black women and female children. These two modes of spiritually-based cultural and social advocacy complement one another. Black male believers must spiritually grow to envision Black Sisters as **co-equal partners** with sexually righteous Black men in the uplift of Black humanity and community. And as Brothers, we must do all within our power to sexually protect our invaluable female co-strugglers in the work of Black freedom and empowerment.

♦ Cultural Well-being

In the long run, unspiritual, immoral, uncivil, unethnical, unethical, and illegal sexual behavior patterns are not beneficial for the well-being of Black Sisters, for African-American children and families, for our churches and institutions, or for the strong social fabric and cultural excellence of Black people. **Black men who are serious about the Black social struggle do not and will not sexually harm and violate Black women and young girls.** At the end of the day, sexual abuse by Black males on Black females is **incompatible with African-American social advancement**, and with the spiritual attainment of Black believers and churches.

Brothers who are true to the cause of liberation, and who advocate for the cultural, social, and spiritual health of Black people, will respect and sexually protect—and will never sexually mistreat or bring harm to our grandmothers, mothers, sisters, wives, daughters, little girls, and the other females in our cultural experience. Black male believers will behave with sexual and cultural responsibility and integrity. They will become sexually "ethnical" in their relation to Black females, and thereby will offer our Sisters a greater measure of sexual safekeeping, and provide them a better pathway for achieving Black social and cultural success, and for living a Christ-centered faith.

Sexual Integrity of Black Men in Christ

♦ **Living Our Identity**

Black Christian **identity** and **sexual integrity** drive a Brother's commitment to protect his Sisters from sexual abuse. As professing Christians who practice our faith, Black believers embrace Christ as our Creator, Redeemer, and Deliverer from all manner of sin and oppression, including salvation from sexual violence. In the Name of Jesus Christ our Lord, our cultural and spiritual integrity obligates us as Black Christian men to **expose, oppose, cease, remedy,** and **prevent** the sexual abuse of females by the males in our own communities and cultural ranks.

Our identity and integrity as Black men in Christ demand that we stand up against all forms of sexual harm—against sexual actions and behaviors that are illegal, uncivil or criminal; that are unbiblical, unspiritual, immoral; and that are unethical and unethnical. **Integrity** demands that Black Christian men **practice the sexual truth we profess** as biblical believers. It calls us to raise our personal sexual conduct to the standards of holiness revealed in God's Word. Integrity means that Black Brothers cease sexual hypocrisy. In all sexual areas of life, we must become authentic in adhering to our values of Blackness and relationship with Jesus Christ our Lord.

♦ **Making the Commitment**

Integrity leads each of us to make **a personal commitment**. This is the essential starting point. Primarily, every Black Brother should express his commitment with a fervent assertion: **"I don't sexually abuse Black females."**

A Black Brother should declare this affirmation with humility, and with a cautious optimism that bespeaks his personal vulnerabilities in the sexual areas of life. Nevertheless, a Black man in Christ should use this sexual affirmation as his personal point of departure on the spiritual journey of rectifying the social condition of Black male abuse of our Sisters. This is the sexual and cultural commitment required of each Black Christian man who accepts one of the highest moral challenges facing African-American men in our day. **"I don't sexually abuse Black females."**

Each Black Brother has a stake in the matter of the sexual abuse that Black females suffer. **Every** Brother can also make a spiritual choice to take part in alleviating the problem of Black male sexual abusers. **Each** man in Christ—based on his commitment and accountable relationship to the Lord—must take full personal responsibility for preventing sexually abusive behavior in his personal dealings with the women and girls in his relationships. **Each** of us must freely and responsibly choose never to sexually abuse the females in our lives.

♦ **Depending on God**

A Brother who makes this spiritual commitment and declaration should begin to flesh out his word in daily living. Each Brother must understand that all believers possess God's power as the strength we need to turn our sexual profession into practice. As Black Christian men of God, **the Holy Spirit empowers us for actualizing and advancing sexual purity, maturity, and accountability**. A Black Brother's continual victory over sexual sin, and his freedom from committing criminal sexual abuse, lie completely within the power of his own hands and a willing heart that he surrenders to the authority and strength of God. The confident affirmation of a disciple of Christ is sure: *"I can do all things through Christ who strengthens me"* (Philippians 4:13, *NKJV*).

◆ Pushing Back in Public

Another step of integrity calls Black Christian men to **make public statements** against male sexual abuse. Each Brother must take social opportunities to **avow his sexual commitment**. He should openly state his personal stance in the sexual matter of not abusing Black females.

As unashamed Black Brothers, at times we must adamantly express our sexual sentiments, even with a tinge of righteous indignation. We must push back on our Brothers—and on all other males—who instigate or passively tolerate the sexually abusive conduct that males commit on females of African descent. In no uncertain terms, we must confront these detractors. We must stop those proponents or perpetrators of abuse against Black females from getting it twisted.

Whether in the presence of private conversations, professional colleagues, or the public square, each of us must be prepared to make known our courageous affirmation, **"I don't sexually abuse Black females."** Brothers of integrity must push for sexual spirituality, for godlier relationships, between all Black men and Black women.

◆ Teaching Young Men

Black Christian sexual integrity is teachable to **young men.** Black men under God in Christ must work to transform the sexual thinking and behavior of all Black males toward our Sisters in the flesh and in the faith. Black Brothers must especially teach sexual responsibility and accountability to the younger generations of African-American males.[28]

Some Black young men behave in sexually wild ways. They do not have a sexually responsible older Black male to tell them the truth—God's whole biblical truth—about sexual matters of life. They learned their information and values about sex, and how to treat Black females, from street culture, gangs, media images, etc. Sometimes, regretfully, they learned their sexual behavior from watching how another Black male sexually abused their mother. These sexually wayward young Black males did not receive their sexual instructions from Black Christian men of sexual integrity. But they should. **Older Black Brothers must step up to teach sexual integrity to younger Black males, men, and boys**.

◆ Covering All Black Females

Integrity covers **all** Black females from sexual abuse by males— all Sisters must receive the sexual protection provided by the Brothers. Women and senior women, young adult sisters and female adolescents, flowering girls and the very young and innocent female offspring—**all African-American females of every socio-economic class**—all must receive the sexual covering they need and righteously deserve.

We males who are their Brothers in the faith and the flesh must play an essential role in providing this protective covering for all our women. Among all non-Black persons and entities who seek to sexually protect Black females from sexual abuse, Black Christian men must step up to the front of the line to serve any or all our cultural Sisters—the group to which we belong. Whether a Sister is "the least" or "the greatest" in our eyes or society's, God loves her, and desires that we do our cultural part by giving each one full sexual protection.

◆ Guarding Our Daughters

Black Brothers—alongside the presence of our Sisters—must also **teach our daughters** about sexual integrity. We might speak the words below:

"My daughter, no male—no one whoever they are—has a right to sexually misuse and abuse your body. A true Black man will always protect you from those who would sexually hurt you. You, my daughter, are God's child. He created you, and your beautiful body belongs first to Him. With God's help I will do everything within my power to respect and protect you from sexual harm."

◆ Supporting All Women

The work and witness of Black male believers in sexually protecting Black females must mature among our own people, for true love first begins at home with our cultural Sisters. As we grow in our cultural love for Black women, our integrity as Black Christian men will lead us to effectively speak to sexual issues in the wider American society, and in nations and societies across the globe. With greater spiritual strength and conviction, **Black Brothers must add their compassionate voices to the growing calls of diverse women everywhere for protection from male sexual predators.** All female victims of sexual abuse should have access to the spiritual and moral support of the Christ-centered cultural experience of sexually righteous, accountable, compassionate, and protective African-American Brothers.

❧

III.

Corrective
Principles and Practices

||||||||||||||||||||||||||||||||||||||||||||||||||||||||||||||||||||||

5

Seven Sexual Affirmations of a Brother

◇◇

Spiritually-minded Black male believers should demonstrate their sexual integrity as followers of Christ in ways that are **spiritual, moral, civil, ethnical, ethical, legal,** and **protectoral**. Making a firm commitment to act on God's sexual mandate for Black men is the first step we take on the journey of responsible sexual living. It is the foundation that we lay for building a sexually godly way of life.

The actions we pursue most often follow the lead of our spoken words. Thus, pursuing a life of sexual integrity compels a Black

Brother to make an initial assertion of the following positive affirmations. We must first believe and speak a sexual word; our righteous sexual actions will follow.

These sexual affirmations are biblically-based. As a Black Christian man, as one who bases his faith in God's eternal Word, **what is your overall sexual attitude**? Ask yourself, "What are my true feelings about how God's Word speaks and relates to my personal views on sex and Black females?"

The sexual affirmations below will reveal a lot about your sexual ideas toward Sisters. Your response to these affirmations gives an indication of your sexual mind-set and attitude. As a Black Christian man, you can measure your overall **attitude toward Bible-based sexual values** by reflecting on these affirmations and their Scripture bases. You can also position yourself as a Black male to personally prevent any sexual abuse you may be thinking of perpetrating on a Sister.

In the words below, I encourage each Brother to specifically affirm what it means for him to be sexually **spiritual**, **moral**, **civil**, **ethnical**, **ethical**, **legal**, and **protectoral**.

Declaring
Seven Biblically-based
Positive Sexual Affirmations

---

1) † "I am sexually **spiritual**."

- I am keeping a clean spirit by living sexually sanctified through God's Holy Spirit. I believe in pleasing God, consecrating females, and obeying God's will for the sexual areas of life.

◊ **Reflect**: *"³ For this is the will of God, your sanctification: that you abstain from sexual immorality ; . . . ⁷ For God did not call us to impurity, but in holiness. ⁸ Therefore the one who rejects this is not rejecting man, but God, who also gives his Holy Spirit to you"* (1 Thessalonians 4:3, 7-8, *LEB*).

◊ **Reflect:** *"⁵ Therefore put to death what is earthly in you: sexual immorality, uncleanness, lustful passion, evil desire, and greediness, which is idolatry"* (Colossians 3:5, *LEB*).

◊ **Reflect:** *"²³ Now may the God of peace himself sanctify you completely, and may your spirit and soul and body be kept complete, blameless at the coming of our Lord Jesus Christ. ²⁴ The one who calls you is faithful, who also will do this"* (1 Thessalonians 5:23-24, *LEB*).

༄

```
┌─────────────────────────────────────────────┐
│         2) † "I am sexually moral."           │
└─────────────────────────────────────────────┘
```

- In the privacy of my thoughts, in my character, and in my public conduct, I maintain right, good, and high sexual values according to biblical standards that govern relationships between males and females.

◊ **Reflect:** *"When you follow the desires of your sinful nature, the results are very clear: sexual immorality, impurity, lustful pleasures"* (Galatians 5:19, *NLT*).

◊ **Reflect:** *"¹It is actually reported that there is sexual immorality among you, and of a kind that even pagans do not tolerate: A man is sleeping with his father's wife. ²And you are proud! Shouldn't you rather have gone into mourning and have put out of your fellowship the man who has been doing this?"* (1 Corinthians 5:1-2, *NIV*).

◊ **Reflect:** *"⁹Don't you realize that those who do wrong will not inherit the Kingdom of God? Don't fool yourselves. Those who indulge in sexual sin, or who worship idols, or commit adultery, or are male prostitutes, or practice homosexuality"* (1 Corinthians 6:9, *NLT*).

◊ **Reflect:** *"Marriage should be honored by all, and the marriage bed kept pure, for God will judge the adulterer and all the sexually immoral"* (Hebrews 13:4, *NIV*).

ℰↄ

3) † "I am sexually **civil**."

- In my conversations, digital expressions, and personal interactions, I keep my communication sexually decent and above sexual vulgarity. I maintain respectful sexual manners by avoiding any kind of lewd or indecent sexual acts or behavior, especially in the presence of elderly women, our "mothers." I do not stalk females. I stay within sexually appropriate and legally civil boundaries.

◊ **Reflect:** *"³ You have had enough in the past of the evil things that godless people enjoy—their immorality and lust, their feasting and drunkenness and wild parties, and their terrible worship of idols. ⁴ Of course, your former friends are surprised when you no longer plunge into the flood of wild and destructive things they do. So they slander you. ⁵ But remember that they will have to face God, who stands ready to judge everyone, both the living and the dead"* (1 Peter 4:3-5, *NLT*).

◊ **Reflect:** *"³ But among you there must not be even a hint of sexual immorality, or of any kind of impurity, or of greed, because these are improper for God's holy people. ⁴ Nor should there be obscenity, foolish talk or coarse joking, which are out of place, but rather thanksgiving"* (Ephesians 5:3-4, *NIV*).

℘

4) † "I am sexually **ethnical**."

- I speak with and treat Sisters of African descent with sexual sacredness, respect, and community. I strengthen my people by sexually uplifting women, younger females, and girls in my own ethno-cultural group. If single, I live sexually responsible and will seek God's guidance to seriously consider taking steps to marry a Sister as soon as possible. I will stay faithful to my spouse as my intimate sexual companion, as my Sister.

◊ **Reflect:** *"⁷ When Boaz had finished eating and drinking and was in good spirits, he went over to lie down at the far end of the grain pile. Ruth approached quietly, uncovered his feet and lay down. ⁸ In the middle of the night something startled the man; he turned—and there was a woman lying at his feet! ⁹ 'Who are you?' he asked. 'I am your servant Ruth,' she said. 'Spread the corner of your garment over me, since you are a guardian-redeemer of our family.' ¹⁰ 'The LORD bless you, my daughter,' he replied. 'This kindness is greater than that which you showed earlier: You have not run after the younger men, whether rich or poor. ¹¹ And now, my daughter, don't be afraid. I will do for you all you ask. All the people of my town know that you are a woman of noble character. ¹² Although it is true that I am a guardian-redeemer of our family, there is another who is more closely related than I. ¹³ Stay here for the night, and in the morning if he wants to do his duty as your guardian-redeemer, good; let him redeem you. But if he is not willing, as surely as the LORD lives I will do it. Lie* *here until morning.' ¹⁴ So she lay at his feet until morning, but got up before anyone could be recognized; and he said, 'No one must know that a woman came to the threshing floor'"* (Ruth 3:7-14, *NIV*).

℘

5) † "I am sexually **ethical**."

- In professional, private, or public settings, I keep a principled and appropriate sexual distance and relationship between females and myself. I seek to create and maintain an atmosphere and environment of sexual morality in the social spaces for which I am responsible.

◊ **Reflect:** *"¹Do not rebuke an older man harshly, but exhort him as if he were your father. Treat younger men as brothers, ² older women as mothers, and younger women as sisters, with absolute purity"* (1 Timothy 5:1-2, *NIV*).

◊ **Reflect:** *"Don't let anyone look down on you because you are young, but set an example for the believers in speech, in conduct, in love, in faith and in purity"* (1 Timothy 4:12, *NIV*).

◊ **Reflect:** *"For the rest, brethren, whatever is true, whatever is worthy of reverence and is honorable and seemly, whatever is just, whatever is pure, whatever is lovely and lovable, whatever is kind and winsome and gracious, if there is any virtue and excellence, if there is anything worthy of praise, think on and weigh and take account of these things [fix your minds on them]"* (Philippians 4:8, *ANT*).

ര

6) † "I am sexually **legal**."

- I keep all my sexual activities and practices within lawful boundaries, and will especially guard myself from committing legally uncivil or criminal sexual behavior against my Sisters.

◊ **Reflect:** *"⁸Now we know that the law is good, if one uses it lawfully, ⁹understanding this, that the law is not laid down for the just but for the lawless and disobedient, for the ungodly and sinners, for the unholy and profane, for those who strike their fathers and mothers, for murderers, ¹⁰the sexually immoral, men who practice homosexuality, enslavers, liars, perjurers, and whatever else is contrary to sound doctrine, ¹¹in accordance with the gospel of the glory of the blessed God with which I have been entrusted"* (1 Timothy 1:8-11, *ESV*).

◊ **Reflect:** *"¹¹But when [Tamar] brought them near him to eat, [Amnon] took hold of her and said to her, 'Come, lie with me, my sister.' ¹²She answered him, 'No, my brother, do not violate me, for such a thing is not done in Israel; do not do this outrageous thing. ¹³As for me, where could I carry my shame? And as for you, you would be as one of the outrageous fools in Israel. Now therefore, please speak to the king, for he will not withhold me from you.' ¹⁴But he would not listen to her, and being stronger than she, he violated her and lay with her. ¹⁵Then Amnon hated her with very great hatred, so that the hatred with which he hated her was greater than the love with which he had* *loved her. And Amnon said to her, 'Get up! Go!' ¹⁶ But she said to him, 'No, my brother, for this wrong in sending me away is greater than the other that you did to me.' But he would not listen to her. ¹⁷ He called the young man who served him and said, 'Put this woman out of my presence and bolt the door after her'"* (2 Samuel 13:11-17, *ESV*).

෴

7) † "I am sexually **protectoral**."

- I relate to Sisters in a way that is sexually harmless and inoffensive to provide a non-threatening and safe environment for any female in my presence—especially for vulnerable seniors, younger women and little girls—and I am sexually nonabusive and nonviolent.

◊ **Reflect**: *"¹³ Another thing you do: You flood the LORD's altar with tears. You weep and wail because he no longer looks with favor on your offerings or accepts them with pleasure from your hands. ¹⁴ You ask, 'Why?' It is because the LORD is the witness between you and the wife of your youth. You have been unfaithful to her, though she is your partner, the wife of your marriage covenant.*

¹⁵ Has not the one God made you? You belong to him in body and spirit. And what does the one God seek? Godly offspring. So be on your guard, and do not be unfaithful to the wife of your youth.

¹⁶ 'The man who hates and divorces his wife,' says the LORD, the God of Israel, 'does violence to the one he should protect,' says the LORD Almighty.

So be on your guard, and do not be unfaithful" (Malachi 2:13-16, *NIV*).

❧

The seven sexual affirmations above are specific enough to be meaningful and practical. Biblical teachings and the power of God can enable each Brother to affirm these sexual values and standards, and to live with a godly attitude of sexual integrity.

Each affirmation is stated positively, which helps a Brother to maintain a proactive and protective spirit when relating to the females in his life. Potentially, based on his affirmations, every spiritual Brother can testify with sincerity and humility: **"I don't sexually abuse Black females."**

Seven Sexually Protective Practices with Sisters

◇◇

As a Black male believer, you should make a commitment to protect Black females sexually, to protect them by never sexually abusing them. Protective principles can assist every Brother in making and sustaining righteous sexual choices in this area.

The following discussion explains **seven biblical ideas** for preventing you from committing non-criminal or criminal sexual abuse on Black females. These Scripture-based ideas cover sexual **consecration, community, communication, control, conscience, confession,** and **covenant.** As a Black Christian man, you should personally use these God-given principles to sexually guard your Sisters. Also apply them to shield yourself from any sexually-related drama that may lead to your having to face civil or criminal legal repercussions for acting out unwise sexual behavior.

Practicing
Seven Sexually Protective
Principles

First

Practice sexual Consecration as a primary virtue.

"Flee sexual immorality" is a way-of-life instruction for a Christian believer to live sexually clean (see 1 Corinthians 6:18, *NKJV*).

Nurture your own sexual sanctification. Practicing sexual spirituality, morality, celibacy, holiness, sanctification (choose the idea that best suits your understanding)—practicing these godly virtues can close the door on contemplating or perpetrating practices of sexual misconduct, harassment, or assault. **Sexual holiness can shut the door before sexually sinful and illegal practices can even enter the space of your relationships.** By pursuing sexual sanctification, you can roadblock the pathways that lead to criminal sexual abuse. By quitting or avoiding personal sexual activity that is unrighteous or unspiritual, you can stop an illegal form of sexual abuse before it even has a chance to start.

Even though the standards of sexual morality may be dismally low in your social context—"everybody's doing sex"—you can still take a stand for spirituality and sexual godliness. Become sexually sacred. Prior to marriage, choose sexual inactivity—a clean and pure way to live. Biblical standards advocate that followers of Jesus abstain from pre-marital or extramarital sexual activity (see: Hebrews 13:4;

Galatians 5:19-20; Ephesians 5:5-6; 1 Corinthians 5:10-11; 6:9, etc.). According to God's way, find sexual fulfillment with a partner in Christian marriage. Consecrate yourself.

Maintaining good sexually moral and ethical fences are of great personal benefit. They are worth far more than the temporary satisfaction of inappropriate sexual behavior. Consider the emotional pain caused by the social embarrassment that you might receive when a Sister finds it necessary to put you in your sexual place. Or, she may even ignite your prosecution by legal authorities for committing a spontaneous or habitual sexual transgression.

As a Black Brother, you can avoid much sexual drama and danger by always relating in a sacred way to the women in your life.

♣

Second

Promote **Community** in male-female relations.

"Treat . . . younger women as sisters, with absolute purity" (1 Timothy 5:1b, 2b, *NIV*). "Sisters" share family/ community with their "Brothers." Based on this family/ community relationship, the Brothers who influence and lead the Sisters should relate to them in a way that is sexually "pure."

Black men in Christ should encourage and live in **community** with their "Sisters" in the faith, and in the flesh. Genuine love, mutual respect, security, and **trust** are vital ingredients of community. An ethical community leader is a **trustworthy** leader. And a trustworthy leader demonstrates sexual protection for Black females.

Black men who are leaders have tremendous influence and wield great power. As a Black Brother in a leadership position, you easily face a temptation to misuse the power of your status to sexually manipulate or exploit the Black females under the influence of your leadership. Therefore, you should always use a sense of community to guard your relationship with Black females. Sexually protect your Sisters and, in the process, guard your life and leadership position in the community.

When the Enemy tempts you to act toward a Sister in a manner that may be sexually unethical or unethical, pause to seriously consider the implications and consequences. By asking yourself a series of community-related questions you can keep yourself from going to a sexual place with a Sister that is bad for her and you.

Say to yourself, "I am thinking about sexually engaging a Black female who is under my leadership, or within my circle of influence. However, . . ."

- Would I do this sex act with this female if she were my full biological sister?

- Would I want some man to take sexual advantage of my young daughter in a way that is like what I plan to do?

- How would I respond if another man sexually treated my mother in the way that I am about to act?

- What might I do if another leader seduced my wife, like I am trying to seduce this Sister?

- Is my contemplated sexual behavior timely or appropriate for the situation and social context?

- How will my sexual actions affect my Sister's life, and her working relationship with me in the long run?

- In what way could this Sister consider that my sexual expressions are unethical, uncivil, or illegal?

- In what way could my sexual intentions and actions push this Sister too far, causing her to report my behavior as sexual misconduct?

- How could my sexual advances toward this Sister increase my legal and financial exposure?

- What unnecessary risks am I taking in my relationship with this Sister, considering that I could destroy my reputation and send my work or ministry into disrepute?

- By pursuing my intended sexual course with this Sister,

how much can I really afford to lose in terms of my family, close friends, inner peace, or my relationship with God?

A trustworthy Brother does not sexually abuse Black females. He does not sexually violate any female with whom he shares a genuine sense of community. He generally regards all Black women as his "Sisters," and by the virtue of that relationship, he treats these females of African descent with "absolute sexual purity."

♣

Third

Use clear **Communication** on sexual matters.

"Wisdom is the principal thing; Therefore get wisdom. And in all your getting, get understanding" (Proverbs 4:7, *NKJV*).

When men and women deal with sexual issues, few things surpass effective communication. Good discussion is a necessary ingredient in good male-female relationships. A Sister whose nonverbal moves may appear to indicate that she desires from you some immediate expression of sexual passion or love may not at all have that in mind—at least not at that very moment. If you hurry to cross a sexual line because you assume she is saying, "It's okay"—the light is green—you may be making a terrible mistake.

Never assume the sexual intentions of a woman. Sexual sense always warns you to talk and clarify. Ask yourself, "Is she really inviting me closer?" An intimate invite may not really be her intention. Sometimes a woman may be saying "Yes" and "No" at the same time, but about different things. As in, "'Yes,' I would like you to be close. But 'No,' I don't want you to grope and undress me. And I am surely not giving you permission to sexually force me."

As a wise Brother, when it comes to sexual interactions, you should never substitute your "Yes" for her "No." If your courage is right, ask her to explain her cues and nonverbal communication. You may ask, "Are you inviting us into a deeper relationship?" "Tell me, what are your expectations at this time?" You owe it to yourself to be sure. Always get sexual consent before proceeding to sexual intimacy with a Sister.

Communicate to clarify what a Sister is saying sexually—whether she speaks in word or by showing you a clear sign. **Take a woman at her spoken word. Clarify to avoid misunderstanding and sexually violating her.** Discuss sexual matters in a straightforward way to dispel confusion, and to remove any legal grounds for accusations of sexual harassment or assault that she may choose to bring against you later. Talk through sexual inclinations and expectations with a woman—never assume.

Also, **avoid uncivil sexual conversation,** especially in the presence of a female. Bypass lewd and sexually indecent talk. Quit using vulgar language, sexually offensive jokes, disrespectful sexual inferences, and the like. Keep all your sexual communications—written, verbal, digital, pictorial, etc.—aboveboard. Don't allow filthy communication from a sexually dirty mouth to get you into the legal trouble of sexual bullying or harassment. Instead, communicate with respect and sexual courtesy to your female associates.

♣

Fourth

> ## Keep **Control** of your sexual urges and conduct.

*"But if they cannot control themselves, they should marry,
for it is better to marry than to burn with passion"*
(1 Corinthians 7:9, *NIV*).

Having sexual passions is normal for persons who are physically mature and in good health. Strong sexual urges may arise at any time, and unexpectedly. Women are beautiful and very attractive. Gorgeous Black and fervently spiritual women seem irresistible at times, and they abound. Temptations also abound. It is one thing for a male's mind and emotions to turn toward sexual expression when he is in close or private contact with a female. It happens. However, it is quite another thing for a male to begin wading into lustful waters, and to make inappropriate or illicit sexual advances toward a nonconsenting woman.

At one time or another, most every man in Christ has found himself in a situation where he thinks a Sister is leading or enticing him. As men, we enjoy flirtations and seductive titillations. Nevertheless, sexual control says, "Wait" or "Pause." The Word tells a believer to control his sexual expression (see 1 Corinthians 7:1-2, 5, and 9).

> *"3 For this is the will of God, your sanctification: that you should abstain from sexual immorality; 4 that each of you should know how to possess his own vessel in sanctification and honor, 5 not in passion of lust, like the Gentiles who do not know God"* (1 Thessalonians 4:3-5, *NKJV*).

As a Black Christian man, you should avoid being hasty about making a sexual hookup, and you should never cross the forbidden line into sexually harassing a Sister. Depending on the context, by expressing inappropriate sexual interaction—sexual misconduct—you may get yourself into serious trouble, especially if you act out abusive sexual activities in the workplace. Sexually speaking, never go too far too fast.

Any Black Christian man should resist acting out impulsively instinctive-type sexual behavior because a Sister looks good, or wild sexual fantasies have burst upon his psyche. Neither should he allow his sexual passions to warp his thinking about a Sister by taking her and her body for granted. You and a Sister may have had a consensual sexual relationship in the past. However, that past sexual experience does not give you the absolute right to sexually force her in the present. Too many males miss the point and commit date rape.

On a night out, some Brothers abandon control of their lust, and their sexual hormones make them lose their mind. They end up sexually violating a Sister-friend, and their victimized date reports the incident to legal authorities. This leads to charging the Brother with a major sex crime, which he must face for the rest of his life.

"Self-control" is the fruit of God's Spirit (see Galatians 5:22-23). The Word says, *". . . encourage the young men to be self-controlled"* (Titus 2:6, *NIV*). **As Black Christian men, we must learn to control our hands, our hugs, and our sexually tempted hearts.**

Controlling sexual urges relates to a Brother's approach to using protection from sexually transmitted diseases when having sex. Showing humane consideration for the safety of his Black female sexual partner is the issue. Whether a Brother is sexually active as single, married, or in an extra-marital affair—**he is sexually abusive if he spreads a sexually transmitted infection to his intimate partner.** Whenever he poses a health-risk, a responsible Brother will first control his sexual urgencies. Then he will always sexually protect his Sister by using a condom and other measures to protect her health.

♣

Fifth

Follow your **Conscience** in sexual gray areas.

"And though she spoke to Joseph day after day, he refused to go to bed with her or even be with her" (Genesis 39:10, *NIV*).

" [15] They show that the requirements of the law are written on their hearts, their consciences also bearing witness, and their thoughts sometimes accusing them and at other times even defending them.) [16] This will take place on the day when God judges people's secrets through Jesus Christ, as my gospel declares" (Romans 2:15-16, *NIV*).

"Pray for us. We are sure that we have a clear conscience and desire to live honorably in every way" (Hebrews 13:18, *NIV*).

"To the pure, all things are pure, but to those who are corrupted and do not believe, nothing is pure. In fact, both their minds and consciences are corrupted" (Titus 1:15, *NIV*).

Depend on your good conscience to give you guidance in cases when you have questions about how to proceed in your interactions with a Sister. Keeping a good and peaceful conscience, and not being conflicted, are signals that you have integrity and are following the right sexual path in the gray areas of male-female interactions.

You should take time to hear your conscience. No guidelines or principles for sexual behavior can cover every conceivable situation that a Brother may encounter with a Sister. There are many sexually gray areas. In these situations, your conscience can be your guide. And the Holy Spirit working through your conscience reveals all manner of sexual sin, great or small, without or within (cf. John 16:8; Romans 9:1).

Our consciences do not tell us what is ultimately right or wrong. For that information we depend on the truth that the Scripture teaches, not on our consciences. Instead, our consciences tell us to do what we *believe* is right, and to avoid doing what we *think* is wrong. With this distinction in mind, in its proper place our conscience can be our guard and keeper in questionable areas of sexual interaction.

Sometimes your conscience will warn you not to go there in a potential sexual encounter. Your good mind will say, "Don't write that sexually suggestive text message." Or "Don't say those flirtatious words." Or, "You ought not to get too close to her in that situation." Or, "Be careful, your sexual attractions and unsolicited advances might be setting you up for trouble down the road." Your conscience can warn you of sexual danger, if you listen.

Joseph's conscience told him to avoid being alone in the house with the wife of Potiphar, Joseph's master. To her, Joseph was sexually hot, and she tried her best to seduce him. But Joseph kept resisting her adulterous overtures. His sexual principles did not allow him to go there, and his conscience led him to avoid even spending time with her. However, on just one occasion, an unfortunate situation got innocent Joseph into serious trouble. Joseph found himself without any other workers nearby, all alone in the house with Potiphar's wife. When she failed to sexually abuse him, the calculating Sister set Joseph up for sexual abuse accusations, and innocent Joseph ended up in prison. She framed him for criminal sexual abuse. Joseph fell into a sexual trap, despite the warnings of his conscience (see Genesis 39:1-23).

Your conscience can also convict you of sin after you have crossed a sexual line with a Sister. Consider this instance. Sometime after a social or professional encounter with a Sister, you realize that your male sexual conduct has gone a little too far. Perhaps you kissed the Sister when she was not expecting it, or while in the presence of others who perhaps misunderstood your intentions. Or, maybe when parting you touched or embraced her in a way that was sexually inappropriate, only to feel her body's resistance and her emotional disapproval. Maybe you even groped her. By your actions you made "unwanted" and "undesired sexual contact," legal signs of sexual abuse.

On this occasion the Sister may have let the situation pass without confronting you, or making a scene of the matter. However, after the incident you get this gnawing feeling that you have offended the Sister by allowing your sexual passions to misuse her in the situation. Since there were no immediate repercussions—no accusations of sexual misconduct or harassment—you decide to just forget about it. But you can't, and you shouldn't. The reason for your bad feelings is because your **conscience** is kicking in. **Your conscience is convicting you of your sexual transgression**, however seemingly minor or inconsequential.

Male sexual abuse has many manifestations besides overt criminal conduct. A Brother's unspiritual and immoral sexual abuse often need the reproof of a good conscience. All Brothers need the inner witness of a good conscience to correct our sensual and sexual indiscretions, lest these immoral behaviors lead us into sexually abusing Black females in more serious ways, in ways that are illegal and very destructive.

In sexual matters, always keep a good conscience before God and in your dealings with your Sisters.

❧

Sixth

Take **Confession** of sexual sins seriously.

"' 9 Why did you despise the word of the LORD by doing what is evil in his eyes? You struck down Uriah the Hittite with the sword and took his wife to be your own'. . . . 13 Then David said to Nathan, 'I have sinned against the LORD.'" (2 Samuel 12:9, 13, *NIV*).

"He who covers his sins will not prosper, But whoever confesses and forsakes them will have mercy" (Proverbs 28:13, *NKJV*).

Acknowledge your sexual problems and shortcomings to God, yourself, and to any Sister that you have sexually offended.

Let's start with a sexually offended Sister, and let's assume that you have not raped her or committed some other kind of criminal sexual assault against her. Confession is certainly in order in these situations. In addition, in these instances, other responses and repair must accompany sincere contrition—the least of which is honestly facing the legal consequences and remedies for expressing uncivil sexual behavior or committing sexual crimes.

When a Sister closes the door on your unwanted sexual advances (whether they were sexually and legally offensive or not), you should **take time to confess to her your transgression**. Then give her assurances that you will make any necessary inter-relationship adjustments. Promise to do all within your power to prevent the sexual offense from recurring. Clean up your sexual misbehavior, and right the wrongs you did. Sexually repair and make your Sister whole.

Always confess your sins to God. *"⁸ If we say that we have no sin, we deceive ourselves, and the truth is not in us. ⁹ If we confess our sins, He is faithful and just to forgive us our sins and to cleanse us from all unrighteousness. ¹⁰ If we say that we have not sinned, we make Him a liar, and His word is not in us"* (1 John 1:8-10, NKJV). God sees all and knows all; and His reckoning day will come for those who commit sexual sins and violations (see Hebrews 13:4). **Confess your sexual transgressions to God before the time of His judgment.**

King David confessed his sexually abusive sin, adultery with Bathsheba, and his murder of her husband Uriah. He gained the complete forgiveness and mercy of God (see Psalm 32:5-6; 51:1-4ff., and the Psalm 51 Title: "For the director of music. A psalm of David. When the prophet Nathan came to him after David had committed adultery with Bathsheba."). Though not often prosecuted, the act of adultery is illegal in several states. This means that an adulterer can possibly face criminal and civil consequences.[29]

Never forget to confess your sexual sins and shortcomings to yourself. Personally acknowledge your lack of wisdom and sexual self-restraint. Rid yourself of self-deception and self-denial—that you believe yourself to be spiritually stronger than is true in your actual sexual experience. *"Therefore let him who thinks he stands take heed lest he fall"* (1 Corinthians 10:12, *NKJV*; and see 10:13).

Whenever you have already traveled down the path that leads to sexual abuse, confessing your faults is always in order. **Repentant confession can assist your deliverance from sexual sin or**

bondage. This spiritual discipline can help you to establish boundaries against committing sexual harassment or full-scale sexual assault sometime in your future.

❧

```
        ╭─────────────────────╮
        │      Seventh        │
        ╰─────────────────────╯
```

Make a Covenant with your eyes for sexual purity.

"I made a covenant with my eyes not to look lustfully at a young woman" (Job 31:1, *NIV*, and see Job 31:1-4, 9-12).

Emulate the covenant model of sexual fidelity practiced by Job—the ancient and righteous man whom the Lord spiritually tested. Job patiently suffered much loss in his trial, but received God's complete restoration and reward when he passed the test. Like righteous Job, **you can make a real sexual covenant with your eyes to never lust after a woman.**

Each Black Christian man can choose to make a covenant with his eyes. He can make a solemn promise that he will not allow himself to entertain sexually immoral perceptions, thoughts, or abusive sexual behavior. Choose to make this private eye-covenant for sexual cleanness.

Within your heart, make a firm agreement with yourself—a spiritual and sexual compact that you intend to keep—that you will stay sexually pure with your eyes and within your soul—within your inner being. Your eyes are windows into your soul. The covenant that you make with your eyes is like the shade on the window to your soul. A Black Christian man needs a sexually protective shade for his soul, and sexually protective lenses for his eyes.

Jesus gave a warning about male gazes on females, and sexual sin:

" 28 But I say to you that whoever looks at a woman to lust for her has already committed adultery with her in his heart. 29 If your right eye causes you to sin, pluck it out and cast it from you; for it is more profitable for you that one of your members perish, than for your whole body to be cast into hell" (Matthew 5:28-29, *NKJV*).

Jesus continued to speak about the eyes and the inner being:

" 22 The lamp of the body is the eye. If therefore your eye is good, your whole body will be full of light. 23 But if your eye is bad, your whole body will be full of darkness. If therefore the light that is in you is darkness, how great is that darkness!" (Matthew 6:22-23, *NKJV*).

By protecting your eyes from unspiritual gazes, you protect your soul from invasions by sexual temptations. By guarding your soul from sexually immoral ideas (such as pornography or female child porn), you guard your actions from perpetrating any form of sexual abuse. Then, by protecting yourself from engaging in predatory sexual behavior, you are protecting your Sisters from sexual violation. This means that you also are safeguarding your life and future from the legal consequences of committing unethical, uncivil, or criminal sexual activity. This holistic and sexually protective process all starts with the private sexual covenant that you make with your eyes.

It is exclusively your decision to make such a sexual eye-covenant with yourself. My question is one of timing. **When will you make this sexual eye-covenant?** What time is the right and best time for you to make a covenant with your eyes for sexual purity?

I encourage every Black Brother to make this sexual eye-covenant **at his earliest opportunity**. If you have not made the eye-covenant, I suggest that you take a moment to reflect on this topic, to pray, and then to start the covenant process. Do not procrastinate. Be sure that you are for real, that you have prepared yourself, and that you are ready as a Black Christian man to take a sexual stand for the purity of yourself and the protection of the Sisters. Then move yourself to make your commitment.

If you think that you are not yet ready to make the eye-covenant, then ask God to work in you to make you ready. Hear these words, ". . . *work out your own salvation with fear and trembling, [13] for it is God who works in you, both to will and to work for his good pleasure"* (Philippians 2:12b-13, *ESV*).

God is willing, able, and ready to work sexual miracles in the lives of those who are committed to doing His will. The same God whose Word teaches us about the sexual eye-covenant is the same God who supplies the spiritual power to keep the sexual eye-covenant. You can trust God to act in your sexual life by giving you strength for the spiritual journey.

♣

God is Available to Help

You have just read seven practical principles that you can apply to the sexual area of your life. They are: **consecration, community, communication, control, conscience, confession,** and **covenant**. As Black Brothers who practice these virtues, we can strengthen our commitment to check personal sexual abuse. Each of us can choose to prevent our own sexual immorality, misconduct, harassment, or assault of the women we influence, and who lie within our sexual reach. By applying these biblical values and principles as Black Christian men, we can control ourselves from perpetrating immoral and illicit sexual behavior upon any woman in our life.

Each of us can **secure God's help and deliverance over sexual testing and temptations** by claiming the potent promises in His Word:

> *"No temptation has overtaken you that is not common to man. God is faithful, and he will not let you be tempted beyond your ability, but with the temptation he will also provide the way of escape, that you may be able to endure it"* (1 Corinthians 10:13, *ESV*).

Consider an extended rendition of this verse:

> *"For no temptation (no trial regarded as enticing to sin), [no matter how it comes or where it leads] has overtaken you and laid hold on you that is not common to man [that is, no temptation or trial has come to you that is beyond human resistance and that is not adjusted and adapted and belonging to human experience, and such as man can bear]. But God is faithful [to His Word and to His compassionate nature], and He [can be trusted] not to let you be tempted and tried and assayed beyond your ability and*

*strength of resistance and power to endure, but with the
temptation He will [always] also provide the way out (the
means of escape to a landing place), that you may be capable and strong and powerful to bear up under it patiently"
(1 Corinthians 10:13, ANT).*

God is always faithfully present to help a Brother in resisting
the temptation to sexually abuse any female in his life. We can trust
God's power and faithfulness to help us to become and remain sexually responsible and protective.

God stands waiting to assist us as Black Brothers in fulfilling
His divine moral and cultural mandate for protecting Sisters from
sexual abuse by Black males. In this spirit and for this cause, each
of us should choose to make our commitment, **"By God's grace, I
don't sexually abuse Black females."**

❧

Sexual Safekeeping for Sisters and Brothers, to God's Glory

◇◇

Be sure to remind yourself, **Brothers also need sexual protection** from the social and legal consequences of sexually-related violations and drama. The current climate of sexual abuse accusations and allegations can become an unfriendly and challenging sexual atmosphere for any sexually well-meaning African-American Brother. When relating to a Sister—or to any female in the society—you need to construct appropriate sexual fences and defenses to protect yourself. So affirm, **"I don't sexually abuse Black females."** Make this spiritual commitment for yourself as a Brother of sexual integrity—then turn this statement into a fortress for your protection.

Make your sexual affirmation to **guard yourself** from becoming another sexual statistic for committing criminal sexual behavior. Too many Black males have legal issues, or already inhabit the American prison system. You don't need to add yourself to those depressing and defeating numbers. Beware: some law enforcement agencies already unfairly profile Black males. And some persons and employers, professional or otherwise, are already looking for a good excuse to disrupt your employment, and to curtail your social advancement. Charges of sexual abuse, harassment, or assault could be lurking around the next corner of your life. So, guard yourself; keep all your sexual relations safe.

Affirm the sexual safekeeping and well-being of females in your life. Make it for protecting the Sisters from all forms of sexual abuse that appear along the broad spectrum of everything from sexually unspiritual conversation to sexually illegal/criminal conduct. Make your spiritual commitment for the sexual health and healing of misused and violated Black women, female adolescents, and young girls. Make it for their overall progress as mothers and future mothers of our African-American people, of our homes, and of our communities. Make your sexual commitment for your wife, your date, your daughters, your sisters, your aunts, your nieces, your female cousins, your step-girls, your female colleagues, for all your Sisters. In American society, all Black females need a haven.

As Black Brothers we divinely stand in spiritual, cultural, and sexual solidarity with our Sisters, our female friends of African descent. Whether our Sisters have been or are being sexually abused, are at risk of sexual abuse, or are showing themselves to be strong defenders of Black females from male domination and sexual violation—as men in Christ, we Brothers stand in solidarity with our Sisters in their ongoing struggle to be sexually safe and secure as Black females.

Make your spiritual commitment to sexually protect Black females for God's glory. The God we serve is the Creator of humanity and the Father of female sexuality. He is a compassionate and faithful Protector. Our God is the Vindicator of sexually victimized women, and He is their Deliverer from sexual desecration, abuse, oppression, and destructive experience. Jesus our God is certainly our Redeemer, for He freely offers redemptive deliverance from the sins of sexual abuse. His grace and strength grant spiritual transformation for every truly repentant male sexual abuser. The God we serve certainly bestows redemptive love and limitless power upon every sexually violated female, upon all who would by divine favor become an overcoming survivor of the tragedy of sexual abuse.

This God, our Lord, deserves all the praise.

To God be the glory.

May the peace of Christ be with you.

৵

Endnotes

[1] "Approximately 40% of Black women report coercive sexual contact by age eighteen." "Women of Color and Sexual Assault. Percent of Women Raped in Lifetime by Race/Ethnicity: African-American 18.8%, Caucasian 17.9%." Connecticut Alliance To End Sexual Violence, accessed April 21, 2018.
https://endsexualviolencect.org/resources/get-the-facts/women-of-color-and-sexual-assault/

[2] On the conviction of 80-year-old Bill Cosby, see the following:
Eric Levenson and Aaron Cooper, "Bill Cosby guilty on all three counts in indecent assault trial," CNN, April 26, 2018, accessed 4/27/18.
https://www.cnn.com/2018/04/26/us/bill-cosby-trial/index.html
Treva B. Lindsey, "Bill Cosby's guilty verdict was made possible by decades of activism by black women," VOX Media, Apr 26, 2018, accessed 4/27/18.
https://www.vox.com/the-big-idea/2018/4/26/17286932/bill-cosby-2018-trial-verdict-outcome
"In what appears to be a seismic shift in what behavior is tolerated in the workplace, a cascade of high-profile men, many in the entertainment and news media industries, have since been fired or forced to resign after accusations of sexual misconduct that ranged from inappropriate comments to rape." Also, the story lists 28 other men who, short of resignation, experienced fallout such as suspension because of their sexual misconduct. Sarah Almukhtar, Michael Gold and Larry Buchanan, "After Weinstein: 71 Men Accused of Sexual Misconduct and Their Fall from Power," The New York Times, November 10, 2017, updated February 8, 2018, accessed April 21, 2018.
https://www.nytimes.com/interactive/2017/11/10/us/men-accused-sexual-misconduct-weinstein.html
Also, see coverage of the Larry Nassar sexual abuse scandal at Michigan State University. Steve Almasy, "Michigan State president resigns over Nassar scandal," CNN, April 21, 2018, accessed April 21, 2018.
https://www.cnn.com/2018/01/24/us/michigan-state-president-resigns/index.html

[3] Catherine Pearson, Emma Gray, and Alanna Vagianos, "A running list of the women who've accused Donald Trump of sexual misconduct," HUFFPOST, October 8, 2016, accessed April 21, 2018.
https://www.huffingtonpost.com/entry/a-running-list-of-the-

women-whove-accused-donald-trump-of-sexual-misconduct_
us_57ffae1fe4b0162c043a7212

Chris Riotta, "When has Trump been accused of rape or attempted rape? Allegations include a child, his wife, and a business associate," Newsweek, November 26, 2017, accessed April 21, 2018.
http://www.newsweek.com/donald-trump-rape-sexual-assault-minor-wife-business-victims-roy-moore-713531

[4] Roni Caryn Rabin, "As of 1998, an estimated 17.7 million American women had been victims of attempted or completed rape." "Nearly 1 in 5 Women in U.S. Survey Say They Have Been Sexually Assaulted," The New York Times, December 14, 2011, accessed 4/21/18.
http://www.nytimes.com/2011/12/15/health/nearly-1-in-5-women-in-us-survey-report-sexual-assault.html

Rape, Abuse & Incest National Network (RAINN) is the nation's largest anti-sexual violence organization. It carries out programs to prevent sexual violence, help survivors, and ensure that authorities bring perpetrators to justice. Accessed 4/21/18.
https://www.rainn.org/statistics/victims-sexual-violence

See also, Pennsylvania Coalition Against Rape (PCAR), "About sexual violence against women," accessed 4/21/18.
http://www.pcar.org/about-sexual-violence/women

Erika Harrell, Ph.D., "Bureau of Justice Statistics Special Report: Black Victims of Violent Crime," August 2007, accessed 4/21/18.
https://www.bjs.gov/content/pub/pdf/bvvc.pdf

See also, "Statistics about Sexual Violence," National Sexual Violence Resource Center, accessed 4/21/18.
https://www.nsvrc.org/sites/default/files/publications_nsvrc_factsheet_media-packet_statistics-about-sexual-violence_0.pdf

Sexual Assault Prevention and Awareness Center, "1 in 20 women will become targets of stalking behavior at least once during their lifetimes," "What is stalking?" Sexual Assault Prevention and Awareness Center: University of Michigan. Accessed 4/21/18.
https://sapac.umich.edu/article/65

[5] See the Times Up movement, "Powerful Hollywood Women Unveil Anti-Harassment Action Plan," January 1, 2018. Among their initiatives: a $13 million legal defense fund, administered by the National Women's Law Center, to support lower-income women seeking justice for sexual harassment and assault in the workplace; and advocating for legislation to punish companies that tolerate persistent harassment. Accessed 4/21/18.
https://www.timesupnow.com/

[6] In this discussion, "Brothers" usually indicates Black Christian men, or African-American male believers. "Sisters" mostly indicates Black women/females or American females of African descent, but sometimes it indicates Black females who are Christian. In either case, see the use of these terms in their context.

[7] See Karen Attiah, *"The Washington Post's* global opinions editor, says current conversation surrounding sexual harassment largely excludes victims who are women of color." "When Black women's stories of sexual abuse are excluded from the national narrative," Weekend Edition Sunday, National Public Radio (NPR), WBEZ Chicago, December 3, 2017, accessed 4/21/18.
   https://www.npr.org/2017/12/03/568133048/women-of-color-and-sexual-harassment
Clarissa Hamlin, "Here's why only a few women of color report sexual assault," Newsone, November 20, 2017, accessed 4/21/18.
Clarissa Hamlin states, "Why are stories of sexual assault told by women of color rarely corroborated by society? In the chorus of women who have recently come forward about abuse in Hollywood, the voices of Black, Latino and Asian women have not been raised above whispers. A demonizing pattern of social conditioning, based on racism, has tainted the images of women of color, especially Black females." "Here's why only a few women of color report sexual assault," Newsone, November 20, 2017, accessed 4/21/18.
   https://newsone.com/3760225/reporting-sexual-assault-black-women-weinstein-lupita-nyongo-tarana-burke-women-color/

[8] Clarissa Hamlin, "It is this damning socialization that first found roots in slavery. Black women's bodies were used and abused without regard to any degree of humanity." "Here's why only a few women of color report sexual assault," Newsone, November 20, 2017, accessed 4/21/18.
   https://newsone.com/3760225/reporting-sexual-assault-black-women-weinstein-lupita-nyongo-tarana-burke-women-color/

[9] Note the white push back against sexually abused Black females. Karen Attiah states, "Not only is there a sense of we're excluded from the narrative, but even when prominent members of our community are in the narrative, that we're the ones whose stories are pushed back upon. We're the ones who are lying." Women of color and sexual harassment, National Public Radio, December 3, 2017, accessed 4/21/18.
   https://www.npr.org/2017/12/03/568133048/women-of-color-and-sexual-harassment

See the experience of Lupita Nyong'o, "Speaking Out about Harvey Weinstein," The New York Times, Opinion, October 19, 2017, accessed 4/21/18.
https://www.nytimes.com/2017/10/19/opinion/lupita-nyongo-harvey-weinstein.html?_r=0

[10] The Recy Taylor story, most recently highlighted by Oprah Winfrey, says it all. Six white men gang-raped the African-American mother in 1944, and two all-male white juries twice acquitted her assailants, despite their confession to the sexual assault. In 2011, the State of Alabama apologized to her for its failure to prosecute her attackers. "Recy Taylor," Wikipedia, accessed 4/21/18.
https://en.wikipedia.org/wiki/Recy_Taylor

Also note the following: "Long before the Cosby trial, black women paved the way for our current robust national conversation about sexual violence." "Indeed, it's important to recognize that years of black women's anti-rape and anti-sexual assault activism have helped produce our current robust national conversation about sexual violence. **It may not be a full moment of reckoning just yet**, but the tireless organizing of black women has made it possible for us to have more productive conversations about rape culture and the meaning of consent." [emphasis added]

Treva B. Lindsey, "Bill Cosby's guilty verdict was made possible by decades of activism by black women," VOX Media, Apr 26, 2018, accessed 4/27/18.
https://www.vox.com/the-big-idea/2018/4/26/17286932/bill-cosby-2018-trial-verdict-outcome

[11] Steve Reilly, "Tens of thousands of rape kits go untested across USA." "Exclusive nationwide count by USA Today reveals abandoned rape evidence," USA Today, July 16, 2015, accessed 4/21/18.
https://www.usatoday.com/story/news/2015/07/16/untested-rape-kits-evidence-across-usa/29902199/

END THE BACKLOG is a program of the Joyful Heart Foundation and supporter of the NO MORE movement. Accessed 4/21/18.
http://www.endthebacklog.org/backlog-what-it/defining-rape-kit-backlog.

[12] End Sexual Violence, "PERCENT OF WOMEN RAPED IN LIFETIME BY RACE/ETHNICITY," accessed 4/21/18.
https://endsexualviolencect.org/resources/get-the-facts/women-of-color-and-sexual-assault/

Aabye-Gayle Francis-Favilla, "Remaining anonymous as a victim of sexual assault is common. And, black women are even less likely than their white counterparts to report that they've been raped."

"'You Are Not Alone:' Uncovering the Dark Secret of Black Women
and Sexual Abuse" in The Body Is Not An Apology (TBINAA), March
29, 2017, accessed 4/21/18.
https://thebodyisnotanapology.com/magazine/a-dark-secret-
sexual-assault-african-american-women/
[13] See Just Be Inc, and the "Me Too" movement. Tarana Burke created
the "Me too" slogan to raise awareness of the pervasiveness of sexual
abuse and assault in society and has said it's partly about "survivors
talking to survivors" and "exchanging empathy." "Tarana Burke,"
Wikipedia, accessed 4/21/18.
https://en.wikipedia.org/wiki/Tarana_Burke
Just Be Inc, Wikipedia, accessed 4/21/18.
http://justbeinc.wixsite.com/justbeinc/home
"Me Too (hashtag)," accessed 4/21/18.
https://en.wikipedia.org/wiki/Me_Too_(hashtag)
In 2017, actress Alyssa Milano started using "Me too" as an Internet
hashtag in response to accusations against several public figures of
sexual harassment, sexual assault, and other abusive behavior.
See Black Sexual Abuse Survivors (BSAS) and their support system
for African-Americans, which serves as an online support group
for black, adult males and females who experienced sexual abuse
as children. Sylvia Coleman, an African-American sexual abuse
survivor and national sexual abuse prevention expert, founded the
nonprofit group in 2008. Accessed 4/21/18.
http://www.blacksurvivors.org/home.html
See also, "Sexual abuse," Wikipedia, accessed 4/21/18.
https://en.wikipedia.org/wiki/Sexual_abuse#Minorities
See also, RAINN (Rape, Abuse & Incest National Network), accessed
4/21/18.
https://www.rainn.org/about-rainn
[14] Dahleen Glanton, "Can the #MeToo movement free black men of the
sexual predator stereotype?" Chicago Tribune, December 11, 2017,
accessed 4/21/18.
http://www.chicagotribune.com/news/columnists/glanton/ct-met-
glanton-metoo-black-men-20171211-story.html
[15] Black Survivors, "Verbal and non-verbal cultural messages that foster
abuse in the Black community," December 12, 2017, accessed 4/21/18.
See also, Robin D. Stone, "No secrets no lies: How Black families can
heal from sexual abuse."
http://www.blacksurvivors.org/aa_and_sexual_abuse.html
Aabye-Gayle Francis-Favilla, "It is important that this trend [to blame
the victim] change, however, because the cost of silence is high.

Rape victims commonly suffer from a number of symptoms post attack. These can include, but are not limited to: denial, withdrawal, depression, chronic anxiety, or alcohol abuse/dependence. Sexual assault can also lead to an unplanned pregnancy or an STD. Can you imagine going through any of those things and not having a safe space to share your experience? It would only exacerbate your suffering. It is important that victims not feel isolated. It is our job to make them feel heard and safe." "A dark secret: Sexual assault of African American women," The Body Is Not an Apology, March 29, 2017, accessed 4/21/18. https://thebodyisnotanapology.com/magazine/a-dark-secret-sexual-assault-african-american-women/

[16] Cherise Charleswell, "Black women have been conditioned to be their brother's keepers—and have allowed themselves to be perpetual victims by doing so." "Sexual abuse and the code of silence in the Black community," Culture and Politics, Role Reboot, September 8, 2014, accessed 4/21/18. http://www.rolereboot.org/culture-and-politics/details/2014-09-sexual-abuse-code-silence-black-community/

Lauren Rosenblatt, "Why it's harder for African American women to report campus sexual assaults, even at mostly black schools," Q&A Politics, The Los Angeles Times, August 28. 2017, accessed 4/21/18. http://beta.latimes.com/politics/la-na-pol-black-women-sexual-assault-20170828-story.html

Aabye-Gayle Francis-Favilla, "'You Are Not Alone:' Uncovering the Dark Secret of Black Women and Sexual Abuse," March 29, 2017, accessed 4/21/18. https://thebodyisnotanapology.com/magazine/a-dark-secret-sexual-assault-african-american-women/

Women ages 18-24 who are college students are three times more likely than women in general to experience sexual violence. RAINN, accessed 4/21/18. https://www.rainn.org/statistics/victims-sexual-violence

[17] Refer to a few of the many sources:
"Sexual abuse," Wikipedia, accessed 4/21/18. https://en.wikipedia.org/wiki/Sexual_abuse
"Legal definition of sexual abuse," Merriam-Webster's Collegiate Dictionary, accessed 4/21/18. https://www.merriam-webster.com/legal/sexual%20abuse
American Psychological Association (APA), "Psychological topics: sexual abuse," accessed 4/21/18. http://www.apa.org/topics/sexual-abuse/

See the following source for helpful definitions of sexual abuse,
Lipscomb University, "Sexual misconduct prevention: Title IX
definitions," accessed 4/21/18.
https://www.lipscomb.edu/safety/sexual-misconduct-prevention/
title-ix-definitions
See, nafisa@thatxxv, on the meaning of sexual consent and rape, see
the $5 metaphor in a tweet, "I don't get how rape is so hard to
understand for some men. But, if you put it like this, they get it."
August 16, 2016, accessed 4/21/18.
https://twitter.com/thatxxv/status/765559476694847488
On "sexual consent" see also, the University of Iowa, Operations
Manual, "Ch.2 - Sexual Misconduct, Dating/Domestic Violence,
or Stalking Involving Students," "2.3 Definitions and Examples of
Sexual Misconduct," "Consent definition." Accessed 4/21/18.
https://opsmanual.uiowa.edu/students/sexual-misconduct-
datingdomestic-violence-or-stalking-involving-students/
definitions-and-1

[18] See the current state laws on marital rape. "Marital rape," Wikipedia,
accessed 4/21/18.
https://en.wikipedia.org/wiki/Marital_rape_(United_States_law)

[19] "Several sexual abuse scandals have involved abuse of religious
authority and often cover-up among non-abusers, including cases in
the Southern Baptist religion, Catholic Church, Episcopalian religion,
Islam, Jehovah's Witnesses, Lutheran church, Methodist Church, The
Church of Jesus Christ of Latter-day Saints, the Fundamentalist Church
of Jesus Christ of Latter Day Saints, Orthodox Judaism, other branches
of Judaism, and various cults." "Sexual abuse," Wikipedia, accessed
4/21/18.
https://en.wikipedia.org/wiki/Sexual_abuse#Minorities

[20] Sexual abuse has a myriad of consequences in the following areas:
physical, psychological, social, and health risk behaviors. "Sexual
violence can have harmful and lasting consequences for victims,
families, and communities." See the extensive list of consequences
provided: "Sexual Violence: Consequences," Centers for Disease
Control and Prevention (CDC), accessed 4/21/18.
https://www.cdc.gov/violenceprevention/sexualviolence/
consequences.html
American Psychological Association (APA), "Immediate reactions to
sexual abuse include shock, fear or disbelief. Long-term symptoms
include anxiety, fear or post-traumatic stress disorder." "Psychology
Topics:Sexual Abuse," accessed 4/21/18.
http://www.apa.org/topics/sexual-abuse/

Devonae Robinson, "The analysis of the literature revealed that there are substantial differences across ethnic groups following sexual assault that can be observed at **the cultural, psychological, and social levels**" (emphasis added). See, "Ethnic Differences in the Experiences of Sexual Assault Victims," OPUS, New York University (NYU) Steinhardt, Department of Applied Psychology, accessed 4/21/18.
https://steinhardt.nyu.edu/appsych/opus/issues/2015/spring/robinson

"Sexual violence can have long-term effects on victims," RAINN, accessed 4/21/18.
https://www.rainn.org/statistics/victims-sexual-violence

[21] See the words of Jesus in Matthew 5:28-29 about gazes that are lustful and adulterous.

[22] Samantha Allen, "Marital rape is illegal everywhere in the U.S. but the cultural and legal obstacles facing its victims remain formidable." "Wedlock," in The Daily Beast, June 9, 2015, accessed 4/21/18.
https://www.thedailybeast.com/marital-rape-is-semi-legal-in-8-states

[23] In some cases, participating in unprotected sex is criminal. See Kristena Ducre's state-by-state breakdown of the penalties for such crimes, "It's the law: Disclosing a positive HIV status," in Exposed: STDCheck.com (blog). June 22, 2015, accessed 4/21/18.
https://www.stdcheck.com/blog/hiv-law-disclosure/

See also, Patrick McGreevy, "Having unprotected sex without telling partner about HIV-positive status no longer would be a felony under new bill." The Los Angeles Times, March 17, 2017, accessed 4/21/18.
http://beta.latimes.com/politics/la-pol-sac-aids-felony-20170315-story.html

[24] Dominique A. Simons, "However, classifying sexual offenders has been shown to be problematic." Sex Offender Management Assessment and Planning Initiative (SMART), Office of Justice Programs; Office of Sex Offender Sentencing, Monitoring, Apprehending, Registering, and Tracking. Chapter 3: Sex Offender Typologies. Accessed 4/21/18.
https://www.smart.gov/SOMAPI/sec1/ch3_typology.html

[25] "While efforts to treat sex offenders remain unpromising, psychological interventions for survivors — especially group therapy — appears effective." Adapted from the Encyclopedia of Psychology. American Medical Association, accessed 4/21/18.
http://www.apa.org/topics/sexual-abuse/

[26] "The treatment of sexual offending behaviors is complex . . ."

"Pharmacological Interventions With Adult Male Sexual Offenders". Association for the Treatment of Sexual Abusers (ATSA) Adopted by the ATSA Executive Board of Directors August 2012. ATSA is an international, interdisciplinary, nonprofit organization dedicated to making society safer by preventing sexual abuse.

http://www.atsa.com/pharmacological-interventions-adult-male-sexual-offenders   accessed 4/21/18.

Michael Hubbard, "Sex offender therapy is challenging regardless of the nature of the clients, and other factors also come into play. There exists the constant issue of resistance to treatment, particularly when treatment is a condition of probation or parole." "Sex offender therapy: A battle on multiple fronts," Counseling Today, Member Insights, Opinion.

http://ct.counseling.org/2014/03/sex-offender-therapy-a-battle-on-multiple-fronts/   March 31, 2014, Accessed 4/21/18.

[27] Trevor Hoppe, "Punishing sex: Sex offenders and the missing punitive turn in sexuality studies," Law & Social Inquiry, 41:3, Summer 2016, 573-94. DOI: 10.1111/lsi.12189. "One percent of all black men in the U.S. are registered sex offenders, and black men enter the sex offender registry at nearly twice the rate of white men . . ." The *research contends that sex offender registries reflect widespread, systemic bias.* See the study cited below:

https://www.albany.edu/news/69837.php , which cites the following study: "Criminal stereotype of African Americans," accessed 4/21/18.

http://onlinelibrary.wiley.com/doi/10.1111/lsi.12189/abstract May 19, 2016, Accessed 4/21/18.

https://en.wikipedia.org/wiki/Criminal_stereotype_of African_ Americans

[28] Wise King Solomon taught his son sexual integrity based on God's standards and ancient African wisdom. We find this extensive teaching in the book of Proverbs. In some ways, Solomon was a sexual failure. But he learned from experience. Time and again, in passage after passage, we learn Solomon's practical teaching on how young men should sexually relate to women, at least in certain situations (see Proverbs 2:16ff.; 5:1ff., 15ff.; 6:24ff.; 7:5ff.; 23:27-28, etc.). As Black Christian Brothers we can integrate the instructions of Solomon into what we teach our sons, nephews, and other younger males about sexual matters.

[29] As of 2018, "adultery remains a criminal offense in 21 states, but prosecutions are rare." Accessed 4/21/18.

https://en.wikipedia.org/wiki/Adultery

About The Author

Rev. Dr. Walter Arthur McCray is a Gospelizer, a holistic *"Good News" messenger* of the resurrected Lord, Jesus Christ. He is a Chicago-based writer and entrepreneur, a seasoned servant-leader in the Church, and president of the National Black Evangelical Association (Chicago). **Dr. McCray** and his wife of 40+ years have several spiritual children and Godchildren.

Contact:

773.826.7790

info@blacklightfellowship.com

https://www.blacklightfellowship.com

BLACK LIGHT FELLOWSHIP
A Beacon of Christ

www.ingramcontent.com/pod-product-compliance
Lightning Source LLC
Chambersburg PA
CBHW072149020426
42334CB00018B/1930